TURBULENCE

TURBULENCE

LEADERSHIP'S UNSEXY
SOLUTION TO STREAMLINE
RAPID GROWTH

MONIQUE MALEY

LIONCREST

PUBLISHING

TURBULENCE

Leadership's Unsexy Solution to Streamline Rapid Growth

ISBN   978-1-5445-2346-0   *Hardcover*

978-1-5445-2345-3   *Paperback*

978-1-5445-2344-6   *Ebook*

For Lucca, who both challenges and inspires me to continually grow in my most demanding and most important leadership role.

CONTENTS

INTRODUCTION

"Anyone can helm when the sea is calm."

—PUBLILIUS SYRUS

If you have flown in an airplane, you have most likely experienced turbulence. You're cruising along reading a book, eating pretzels, and sipping ginger ale (or in my case, a Bloody Mary), when suddenly the plane starts shaking and jumping around, threatening to send that ginger ale straight into your lap.

No matter where you're sitting on the plane, you feel the unsettling movement. If there's an eddy under the right wing and you're sitting on the left side or in the back, you'll still feel it. And if you look out the window to find the source, you likely won't see a thing.

Pilots use radar to avoid rough patches, and planes are designed to streak through the air, getting us from point A to point B with minimal bouncing, yet even the best pilots and aerodynamics cannot completely eliminate turbulence. At some point, it will show up, sometimes unexpectedly, and it will slow the trip or divert the plane, causing delays and frustrated or unhappy passengers. Pilots do what they can to handle it most effectively, streamlining the experience for those on board. Knowing how to avoid, manage, and mitigate the choppiness and disruption is an essential part of their job.

In many ways, businesses are like airplanes: they all experience turbulence. It doesn't matter if it's a newer company that has recently taken off or an older organization that has reached cruising altitude—shaking and discomfort happen.

Technology and access to capital allow companies in today's world to grow faster than ever. Unfortunately, leaders' ability to iterate and learn to lead during rapid growth often cannot keep pace with their organization's needs. This opens the door to turbulence on many levels. Like passengers on a jet, employees, clients, even board members feel the bumps, no matter the source of disruption or where those stakeholders fit in the organization. Like pilots, leaders are ultimately up front on their own, and it's their responsibility to pinpoint, address, and alter course to minimize the instability. This takes time, awareness, and acting with intention, especially if leaders themselves are the cause of the disruptions.

As on planes, turbulence in an organization causes slowdowns, unhappy stakeholders, and delays. It can also cause low morale, lack of retention, slowed sales, and challenging board relationships, to name a few. In the end, not taking time to identify and streamline these areas of disruption will cost leaders and their organizations more time, money, productivity, and ultimately growth.

AT THE CORE

When teams or whole organizations experience unsteadiness or a drag on growth, it's natural for leaders to look for an external source that can be avoided or at least mitigated. You might be aware of challenges resulting from a lack of investor funding, changes in the market, improved systems architecture, or even a global pandemic.

This book cannot provide answers for every shift in the trade winds. It is not a one-stop shop for all leadership or rapid-growth challenges. Instead, my aim is to help you identify, reframe, and manage issues at the core of turbulence that are often related to an underestimated facet of leadership.

Communication.

I know, communication is not sexy. After ten years working in this space, I am very aware that no one wakes up in the morning and says, "Hey, today I want to become a better communicator." But you might say, "I need to make sure my board is with me," or "I've got to get my team to finish this project on time," or "I need to close this round of funding." Underlying each of these concerns is your ability to communicate effectively.

Communication is at the core of everything you do as a leader: every conversation with a team member, every job posting and interview, every sales pitch, every staff meeting.

Think of the phrases we often use to describe great leaders: *commanding presence, dynamic energy, inspiring influence.* These words all embody elements of how leaders are perceived and how they inspire and engage. These are all elements of communication. Whether verbal or nonverbal, communication is *the* tool needed to avoid, manage, or mitigate turbulence.

Being able to effectively leverage communication will make you a better leader. Lacking this skill, on the other hand, will inevitably make you an ineffective one, resulting in challenges for you, your team, your organization, and ultimately your growth.

Not yet convinced? You may have had great success to date without intentionally working on your communication; you obviously had the communication skills to get where you are today. However, there will come a time when you need to iterate and expand. There will come a time when your company is growing quickly, and those balls you've been juggling or the plates you've been spinning will fall.

REDEFINING COMMUNICATION

George Bernard Shaw once said, "The single biggest problem in communication is the illusion that it has taken place."

People think that because they've called someone or written an email, they've communicated. Both of these scenarios involve basic exchange of information, which is not the same as communication.

I will say that again: exchange of information is not communication.

Some think they're good at communication because they're slick presenters. Such speakers can come off as condescending and a touch too polished. In the absence of meaningful content that inspires or persuades, overly packaged presentation becomes the message, rather than the intended one.

So what is communication? Let's define it and make sure we're on the same page before we continue.

The word *communication* comes from the Middle English word meaning "to share" or "commune," which means to converse or talk *together*. It involves a dialogue that goes beyond the transmission of information. It is more than mere monologues; it is a "shared" dialogue. Communication involves verbal and nonverbal signals: word choice, tone, body language, facial expression, energy, and more. It is in what you do and don't do. It is in what you say and don't say. It is how you set the tone for a meeting or a culture. It is everything someone else perceives about you or your business, whether or not it is what you intended to convey.

Most leaders don't think of this definition of communication when they look to level up their leadership skills or seek to identify the source of disruption and turbulence in their team or organization. If a company hires a new employee who ultimately doesn't work out, leaders often think the problem is with the new hire, when the issue might actually relate to communication. Perhaps it was a poorly worded job description that appealed to the wrong candidates, or interview questions that didn't help the interviewer identify the right person for the position; maybe it was a lack of clearly communicated expectations. I have seen founding entrepreneurs fail to secure funding and then blame their audience—potential investors' lack of attention or engagement during the pitch or investors who don't "get it"—rather than examine their own clarity, story, or lack thereof. At the core of many workplace problems, like issues with a new hire or a failure to secure funding, is often a leader's inability to communicate vision, confidence, conviction, and more.

HOW THIS BOOK CAN HELP

My goal in writing this book is twofold.

First, I want to increase your awareness of how turbulence shows up in organizations and teams. Think back to the plane metaphor: although everyone onboard feels the shaking, it might be felt more jarringly in the back seats. Pilots might not realize that while they are lightly tightening their seat belts, people in the last row are gripping the armrests and hoping bags don't start falling out of the overhead bins.

As a leader, you feel some disruptions, but you might not even be aware of other rough patches people in your organization are experiencing. It's likely that the farther they are from you, the more acutely they will feel it. If you are unaware, you might not understand how these seemingly small bumps can have widespread destabilizing effects in the organization. I want to help you peel back the layers of the obvious and not-so-obvious challenges to see what's truly at the core. I want to help you become aware of how you're communicating through words, body language, tone, culture, storytelling, and more, and how *you* may be contributing to the turbulence you're facing in your organization, teams, and other stakeholder relationships.

Second, after you gain awareness, I want to give you the tools to assess and reframe your communication, ensuring that you don't continue to contribute to these disruptions and enabling you to begin to make a shift on a daily basis. Because one book could never cover every topic completely, I've also provided numerous resources so you can dig deeper.

Each chapter presents one facet of leadership where ineffective or absent communication can create drag and ultimately turbulence. Together, they cover the most common communications-related challenges experienced by a broad array of leaders I've worked with over the past ten years.

The first chapter starts at the very center of the leader, with internal dialogue; the subsequent chapters radiate out to embrace broader rings of communication. We begin with conversations with ourselves and others, which happen daily and affect everything from confidence, to decision making, to building trust and influence. With each chapter, the audience gets wider, the extent of one's reach extends farther, and the ripples created grow bigger.

For this reason, I recommend reading the chapters in order. The ideas, themes, and strategies in each chapter inform those in the next. After you finish, keep the book handy and come back to it when you start to sense turbulence. Flip through the chapters and try some of the strategies and action items shared. Think of it as a resource that may help you reframe, rethink, and reengage more effectively.

To figure out the true source of turbulence, you have to slow down, assess the situation, and engage with intention. What you might think is a marketing issue or product feature challenge might actually be tied to communication—perhaps an issue with finding common ground or a perceived lack of authenticity. You won't know that until you take a closer look with a fresh perspective.

As with any book, this one does not have all the answers for all people; again, it is not a one-stop shop for every business challenge in a rapidly growing environment. Rather, I offer suggestions for assessing and addressing communication-related disruptions. Likewise, because each organization has a unique combination of people and processes, the strategies offered may smooth the turbulence for some leaders in some situations and not others. My advice: Don't decide whether a tool is right until you take it out of the box and use it. Try at least one strategy and then note the response in other people; this is a solid metric for determining the tool's effectiveness.

If you try a tool and it doesn't work, don't throw it out. It's like sorting through your toolkit to find the right pair of pliers for a particular job or discovering that you actually need a wrench. You'll still keep all the tools in your kit because you may find you need them one day. You might also find that someone on your team needs the very tool that didn't work for you in another context. After all, as a leader, your toolkit is a resource for both you and those you lead.

For those who like statistics, I provide some data that supports the importance of streamlining turbulence, both for the individuals on your team and for the financial health and productivity of your organization as a whole.

For those who learn from stories, I provide Turbulence Alert sidebars with real-life examples and interviews involving individuals who have experienced turbulence in these areas and have seen the benefits of employing the tools presented.

For those who like an actionable to-do list, I provide a Turbulence Toolkit at the end of each chapter that contains questions for self-assessment followed by suggestions for taking intentional action.

MY WHY

Growing and leading a business is hard. It requires capital, both human and financial. It is also lonely. That combination often means leaders in rapidly growing environments rarely make plans or put out fires that are not right in front of them. That isn't a winning formula for success. I should know; I've been there.

I started and grew a luxury beauty and wellness company. By many metrics, mostly financial, it was a success. I had a growing team. We had strong and increasing revenue. Our customers were happy and sang our praises. My employees bought homes and had kids, trusting in the stability and support that the business provided. But ultimately, growth stalled. It didn't fail exactly; it simply plateaued.

In the intervening years, I have spent a great deal of time considering why this happened. Here's what I've concluded:

- I was not leading authentically.
- I engaged with my team personally and warmly but not always effectively.
- I created a culture for growth but only to a point.
- I started with a vision but never fully articulated it, even to myself.
- I hired individuals without ensuring they were aligned and supportive of our mission or culture in deed as well as in word.
- I engaged with clients effectively but never leveraged that engagement for influence.

In short, I was not communicating effectively.

I would not make those same mistakes today, not only because I am older and wiser or because I have actively studied the scientific and sociological research behind leadership or because I have surrounded myself with smart, effective leaders. The ultimate catalyst for change was my willingness to self-assess, be intentional, and work a plan to iterate and grow my leadership.

Now, after more than ten years as president of Articulate Persuasion, I know that whether I am working with a Whole Foods executive or the founder of a fintech startup, the formula for streamlining turbulence is the same: assess, be intentional, work a plan. Now the metrics for my company's success are seen in the goals achieved by my clients, from the $500 million in funding raised to the 57 percent increase in employee retention.

Turbulence: Leadership's Unsexy Solution to Streamline Rapid Growth is the culmination of many years' work, years spent training and working as a professional actor, starting and scaling businesses, learning from my own mistakes, mentoring hundreds of startups, and coaching leaders across industries.

I have seen clients leverage many of these tools and strategies to mitigate and avoid turbulence, all to the benefit of their teams, organizations, and growth. What I love about this work are the outcomes: articulated visions, inspired teams, and authentic leaders, working at their best.

My goal is to create awareness and provide you with a fresh perspective that gives you a way to connect with information and insights you may have missed, forgotten, or simply taken for granted. Then you can become aware of your blind spots, you can craft a plan, and you can iterate your skills to keep pace with your company's rapid growth and needs.

If you're ready to begin, I ask that you be open and give yourself the time and space to process.

We'll start with conversations, the building blocks of all communication.

CHAPTER 1

CONVERSATIONS

DIALOGUE, NOT MONOLOGUE

"A conversation is a dialogue, not a monologue. That's why there are so few good conversations."

—TRUMAN CAPOTE

Communication is like Ping-Pong: neither works if you're the only person playing.

In Ping-Pong, if you serve the ball over the net and no one is standing on the other side to hit it back, the game ends. If no one hits back, there is no game. Likewise, there is no conversation without at least two sides fully engaged and playing. It takes a ping *and* a pong.

As leaders, we go through our day thinking about things we need to do: the email we need to write, the press release that needs to go out, the staff meeting we need to hold. We might see each task as a kind of communication, but we often don't see them as dialogue.

The truth is, if you email a potential customer about a product, that's a dialogue about sales. If you have a meeting with your board of directors, that's a dialogue involving influence and persuasion. If you need to make a big decision on goals for next quarter, that's a dialogue with key players on your team, including yourself. Every conversation, every form of communication, is ultimately a dialogue.

In Ping-Pong, it's easy to imagine the back-and-forth interaction. Both players have a paddle and each hits the ball during the course of the game. In work-related conversations—whether it's a Slack message, a pitch, or a one-on-one discussion—there may not be words coming back from the other side of the net, so to speak, but communication is happening through body language, micro-expressions, energy, tone of voice, word choice, and more. Dialogue is taking place.

For those of you who prefer the theater to Ping-Pong: when a show is running for weeks or months at a time, an actor will do the same play night after night, communing with the audience as they perform. Although the play itself is the same, the actual conversation that takes place between actor and audience differs from night to night. The Friday and Saturday night audiences are usually experienced theatergoers. They may laugh, but it's controlled laughter. The Wednesday matinee is usually full of kids. Their engagement—when they laugh or don't laugh, how much noise they make—communicates to the actor as well but in a very different way than the Friday and Saturday night crowd. In both cases, the audience's responses inform the actor how to return the volley. It's a conversation. It's a dialogue, even if only one person is doing the talking.

When we view any conversation as a monologue instead of a

dialogue, we intentionally or unintentionally make it about us. We limit ourselves to one source of information—ourselves—whether it's one tape in our head or our own perspective during a performance review. We don't really listen and thus miss out on the multitude of messages that can inform our understanding, decisions, and interactions, which ultimately leads to turbulence.

Conversations are an integral part of leading. In the course of a day, they happen hundreds of times across the organization. Some are often labeled "tough" or "crucial" conversations, but many are motivating and informative. If even half of those conversations, whether difficult or positive, are ineffective, happen too late, or don't happen at all, they become a potential source of turbulence in every facet of your company.

To master the skill of effective conversations, we have to begin with the one many leaders find the hardest or often think about the least—conversations with ourselves. I mentioned that leadership can be lonely. This makes effective conversation with yourself essential.

We'll start this chapter by discussing the ways your internal dialogue might be causing challenges for you and your team, along with strategies for stopping those unproductive conversations. Mastering the conversations in your head is the first step to engaging in effective dialogue with people both inside and outside your organization.

CONVERSATIONS WITH OURSELVES

Internal dialogue is sometimes associated with mindset, but it's more. Mindset is the outcome of our thoughts; the internal dialogue is the process that leads to that mindset.

We often talk about mindset when we discuss elite athletes. I am a big fan of professional road racing. In a grand tour, these cyclists race nearly every day for three weeks. Each day lasts four, five, or even six hours without stopping. They race in heat, wind, and freezing rain. They ride fifty miles per hour downhill and up insanely steep mountains—not hills.

How do these cyclists ride up a mountainside after five hours in the rain? Why do they choose to get up and keep going after a brutal fall? Where do they find the power to push to the finish line when they know they can't win the day? How do they lose ground one day and manage to gain the next? Yes, training and skill play a part, but their mindset is the powerful contributor that makes the difference.

Here is where internal dialogue comes into play. They may think, "My legs are burning," or "I'm already past my limit," and then follow those thoughts with, "I've gotten through this before," or "I'm going to win this stage." Jens Voigt, the well-known German cyclist, would famously yell, "Shut up, legs!" as he struggled up a steep climb. The difference between first and tenth place is often mindset. Those who master the art of internal dialogue come out ahead.

TURBULENCE ALERT

Craig was a very successful client of mine who had somewhat plateaued in his own business leadership. For nearly twenty years prior to our working together, he had been a CEO in organizations with limited resources. His internal conversations had revolved around the theme "How do I make the most of what I have?" implying constant scarcity. Craig had never dreamed big because the resources hadn't existed to do so: if he'd made a big request, he would have butted heads with the board of directors or disappointed employees because he promised things he couldn't make happen. Because it had never been a possibility, he had never asked himself, "If I had all the resources I could want at my disposal, what would I do with them?"

Now Craig was CEO of a much bigger company with much deeper resources, both human and financial. He was in a position to think on a grand scale with an almost infinite vision—and that was an unfamiliar place that made him question his judgment. As a result, Craig allowed himself to be informed by other people's ideas as he worked on the strategic plan. After a conversation with one board member, he would come away thinking that was the direction he wanted to go. Then he would talk to someone else—a longtime mentor—and suddenly his vision shifted.

The problem was that Craig never sat down and had a conversation with himself about *his* vision. That wasn't a conversation he was used to having or that he was confident in having.

The goal for Craig was to sit in what felt like discomfort and sort out which perspectives and data points deserved the greatest weight. Out of that came a vision for his organization that was much more exciting, not only for him but also for his employees. Morale skyrocketed.

The goal wasn't to outright dismiss those other ideas but to understand who was contributing to the conversation and to make sure his own voice was the strongest one.

THE TAPES IN YOUR HEAD

Having an effective conversation with yourself is not necessarily about eliminating unproductive or even negative thoughts. It's about having a dialogue, not a monologue, with yourself in which you give all thoughts their due and then choose which perspective deserves more weight. If you think about your mind as a conference room, that means giving every perspective at the table the space to speak, not just the loudest or the most negative.

One-sided conversations with yourself are as unproductive and occasionally as damaging as one-sided conversations with others. They are influenced by your beliefs, your experiences, your mood, as well as the tapes you have running through your head. Some tapes may come from a mentor, a dominating board member, or even someone you worked with years ago. Although you need to be aware of the valid points those tapes bring to the dialogue, you also need to recognize when they have no place in the conversation or in what you're trying to achieve. More often than not, in allowing other voices to dominate, you become the biggest obstacle to your own successful leadership.

Whether positive or negative, the tapes from our past are now part of our internal dialogue and affect nearly every aspect of our leadership: our mindset, our confidence, our credibility, and for entrepreneurial leaders, our risk tolerance. The skill to master is knowing which tapes deserve to be heard and which tapes are just noise. One of my clients has the voice of an early mentor and supporter running through her mind. He saw her promise before she did. Now when she starts to doubt her ability, she lets that confidence-boosting tape play. Another client has the voice of a doubting board member in his head. He used to give this board member's voice all the attention. Now he acknowledges the tape, prepares a rebuttal, and moves on.

To avoid turbulence in this area, it's crucial that you pay attention to the conversations you have with yourself. For example, where do you sell yourself short? What false beliefs do you hold? What blind spots might you be ignoring?

It's also important to understand the source of the information in your dialogue. Is the data coming from a trusted advisor, an experienced team member, or an inner critic? Is it factual or is it all in your head? As suggested in the Streamlining Strategies, it may help to identify the tapes by name and write out their messages to help you discern truth from fiction and to help you decide which voices deserve the most weight.

Internal dialogue forms the most active, impactful, and meaningful conversation we have every single day at work. To have more effective conversations with others, to be decisive, and to show up authentically, we have to master our internal dialogue.

STREAMLINING STRATEGIES

It's hard to know when our internal dialogue is causing turbulence for ourselves, our team, and our organization. The following strategies might help you pinpoint where and how the conversations in your head are getting in your way.

Assume Your Internal Dialogue May Be Causing Turbulence

With my clients, I ask questions that invite them to articulate their internal dialogue. I listen for something in the person's inner conversation that may be creating an obstacle for them as a leader individually or within the organization—for example, wording that indicates insecurity or listening to too many ideas from too many contributors. I had a client who was very decisive, but he became tentative when he actually announced the decision because he listened to mental tapes telling him how his team would react. Whether those thoughts were true, they undermined his conviction and caused turbulence for him and his team.

If you start with the assumption that something in your internal dialogue might be creating disruptions for you and your team, you will become more aware of how the issue crops up throughout your day.

Write It Down

As you think through your internal dialogues and start to become aware of related areas of turbulence, write down your insights. I realize not everyone works in pen and paper, but there are many benefits to physically writing things down. Research shows that professionals who write down their goals are 42 percent more likely to achieve them.[1] Other studies show that writing things down helps us focus, with the result being that we are more productive and effective. Writing also allows us to clarify, sharpen our thoughts, and understand complex concepts.[2]

What could be more complex than our internal dialogues? There is something about getting the thoughts out of the spin cycle of our brains and onto paper that allows us to view them with greater clarity and, by extension, more productivity. We're forced to consider: Is that really what I think? Is that really the right thought process? Are those really the most important data points?

---

1 Mary Morrissey, "The Power of Writing Down Your Goals and Dreams," HuffPost, September 14, 2016, https://www.huffpost.com/entry/the-power-of-writing-down_b_12002348.

2 Matt, "The Write Way to Remember: The Power of Writing Things Down," Gr8tness, August 21, 2019, https://www.gr8ness.com/writing-things-down-is-powerful/.

Be aware, however, that typing is not the same as writing. Because typing is faster, our brain has less time to process. Handwriting forces us to slow down and think.

The inner dialogue that leads to imposter syndrome is a common turbulence creator you can address through writing down your thoughts. Imposter syndrome is defined by *Scientific American* as "a pervasive feeling of self-doubt, insecurity or fraudulence *despite* often overwhelming evidence to the contrary."[3] In other words, the internal dialogue dismisses objective proof of leadership qualities, ability to influence, or level of capacity.

We all have in our mind what we think a leader should "look like." If we see ourselves as the outlier or different in any way, we may determine we aren't the real thing. We believe we are an imposter—even if the evidence would say something different.

If a leader has a challenge with imposter syndrome, I have them write down what they think about themself. Nine times out of ten, when they see those thoughts in writing, the person will begin to see what beliefs are real and what are inaccurate.

If you try this and don't see the inaccuracy right away, you still have a list. You can work through each item and ask yourself, "What empirical evidence do I have that affirms this about me?" For example, if a first-time CEO has imposter syndrome and writes "I've never led a team this big," I would ask, "What is it about leading a team this big that somehow makes you feel unprepared?" and have the person write down those thoughts. Those statements likely aren't true; the person simply feels like they are. In psychology, this is known as the "as if," where under-

---

3   Ellen Hendriksen, "What Is Imposter Syndrome?" *Scientific American*, May 27, 2015, https://www.scientificamerican.com/article/what-is-impostor-syndrome/.

standing and personal meaning are based in fundamental ways on fictions—that is, on imaginative or counterfactual beliefs.[4]

The moment you put doubts in writing, you take away their power. They cease to be a reality in your inner dialogue because you see them for what they are.

TURBULENCE-CAUSING INTERNAL DIALOGUE

Imposter syndrome is only one type of turbulence-causing internal dialogue. The following can also get in your way and prevent you from showing up as the leader you need to be.

- *My way or the highway*: "I'm the only one who knows what's best for the company."
- *Mother, may I?*: "I'll double-check with the board to make sure this is a good decision."
- *No help wanted*: "I will get it all done myself."
- *Yes, but...*: "This is a good plan, but I think we need to create a committee to discuss it further."
- *Rose-colored glasses*: "There are no problems here. Everyone loves our brand."

On the other end of that same spectrum, certain leaders' internal dialogue has convinced them they can do no wrong. They think they are the perfect person to scale the company, yet much of the data proves otherwise. For these leaders, writing down internal dialogue will likely not help them avoid or mitigate turbulence because they don't see a need to change. Inaccurate internal dialogue of this nature is just as damaging to the organization.

---

4   Willian E. Smythe, "On the Psychology of 'As If,'" Theory and Psychology 15, no. 3 (June 1, 2005): 283–303.

I have known and worked with some smart founders who helped their companies grow exponentially by having an honest conversation with themselves about hiring a new CEO. An honest internal dialogue about your strengths, your weaknesses, and your vision can help you avoid years of turbulence.

TURBULENCE ALERT

Max had been running a successful business for fifteen years. Prior to the 2020 pandemic, we started working on ways to scale his business. We were deep into this work when COVID hit, and Max had to change his business model to deliver his service in a different way.

The challenge for Max was that in his own mind, his company was not expert in delivering that service virtually. As a result, he unintentionally communicated his worries and fears to his team, so they began to think, "He's worried, so I need to worry" and "We may not make it."

We had to find a way for him to shift the internal conversation around his expertise and, by extension, his offerings. He had to quiet the voice of worry and fear and listen to the voice that laid out the facts and possibilities. Instead of asking himself, "Am I an expert in doing this virtually?" he needed to ask, "If we use our proven process, can we achieve the same results we would have in person? Can we add as much value as we did before? What elements of delivery are the same? Which are easily adapted? How do we manage the rest?"

When Max was able to view virtual as a new tool or delivery method, rather than a completely separate offering, his internal dialogue shifted, and his conversations with others followed. Rather than trying to think of himself as an expert in his virtual service, he started thinking of himself as an expert in the service, which he could provide virtually. This was something he already knew and believed. He simply didn't give these thoughts enough weight. His mindset shift informed the confidence he communicated to his team and his clients. In 2020, Max's business revenue actually grew, and this new offering has provided a second income stream.

Counter with a Different Narrative

Another tactic is to speak aloud statements to actively counter the internal dialogue that is reinforcing a belief. Whatever your particular concern, ask yourself, "What is the counternarrative?" If you don't want that belief coming up in your own mind, what do you need to start saying to yourself to counteract it?

For example, if a leader has an overwhelming conviction when making a decision but they find little to no data or only one perspective to support that conviction, there is likely turbulence on their team. People might feel the leader doesn't listen or doesn't trust their perspective or advice. A counternarrative to a leader's internal "I know I'm right" or "I've done this a million times" might be, "Is there something that makes this time different?" or "Whose point of view have I overlooked?"

Get Out of Your Head

If leadership is lonely, then it gets lonelier the higher up you go. CEOs and other senior leaders have many conversations with themselves because they don't have peers within their own organizations with whom they can converse openly. Organizations like YPO (Young Presidents' Organization), EO (Entrepreneurs' Organization), and Vistage sprang up to meet this need and give leaders a place to actively converse with people who are in the same position and who also spend most of the day keeping thoughts to themselves.

Find or create a group of peers with whom you can have open conversations. Alternatively, hire an executive coach you feel you can trust. The goal is to get these internal dialogues out of your head in a safe and trusted space with people who are not going to tell you what to do but offer perspective. You want a group of peers who give you a place to think out loud so you can start putting that dialogue in context and make sure it's not undermining you. This will also help you create a new inner conversation, one that supports your goals, your company, your vision, your company culture, and the direction in which you're moving.

CONVERSATIONS WITH OTHERS

Once you start mastering your internal dialogue, you can start focusing on your dialogue with others. These conversations include people in every part of your organization: employees, team members, your board as a whole or individual members, clients, and investors.

PEER-TO-PEER CONVERSATIONS

Communication that persuades is effective; communication that doesn't is ineffective. Effective communication with others can only happen when we mentally view the other person as a peer for the duration of that conversation. Figures 1.1, 1.2, and 1.3 illustrate this concept.

When we engage in conversation, whether one-on-one or in a

group, we mentally create a perceived hierarchy and put others in one of three categories. We perceive some people to be (for lack of a better term) above us, such as board members, big clients, or even bullies. We perceive others as being under us, such as students or junior employees. And finally, we perceive some as being on equal footing, whatever their role. It is only in this third place of balanced and equal footing—that is, when we view people as peers—that effective communication takes place. Mentally putting people in the other two categories can create barriers to credibility, active listening, and ultimately, persuasion.

Let's say you are the person on the left in Figure 1.1, and you're trying to communicate with the person on the right, who represents someone you may view as having more power or influence, like your boss, a very important client, or a member of your board of directors—someone you *perceive* as being above you.

Figure 1.1. Communication dynamics with someone perceived as above.

If you engage in conversation with someone and perceive them to be above you, then you have also unwittingly put yourself in a position where that person may *look down on you.* The hierarchy created in your mind will show up in your conversation in one way or another—in your tone, in your body language, in the way you ask questions, in the way you make a statement (or lack of statement). You may well undermine yourself.

For example, if you're in a conversation with an unhappy client whom you perceive as sitting on the top line, you might make a statement like, "Let us fix that for you," which is really a request, as opposed to, "We will fix that for you," which shows much greater surety. In the latter case, you're not asking permission to take care of the situation. You're stating that you will do it. That simple change in wording can create a shift in the dynamic between you.

Figure 1.2. Communication dynamics with someone perceived as below.

Another way we view people in the organization is that they are under us (Figure 1.2). A scientist trying to get buy-in from a lay audience might think of them as being on a lower level or as having insufficient credentials. However, if you view people as being below you—as being less than peers—you will likely be viewed as *talking down to them*. This is never a constructive place for a leader to be with anyone. They may perceive your communication, through tone, body language, and so on, as condescending or dismissive. Condescension and dismissive-ness will taint your message, making it less likely that others will be persuaded.

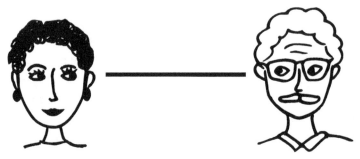

Figure 1.3. Communication dynamics with someone viewed as an equal.

Effective conversation—that is, conversation that secures buy-in and moves people to action—can only happen when we view the other eye to eye, as a peer (Figure 1.3), no matter what their actual position in the company. Dialogue in any conversation is not informed by the actual or perceived hierarchy in the organization or the dynamic with the client or board member. It is informed by how you *view* the dynamics. To this end, I challenge my clients to view each person as a peer for the dura-tion of any given conversation. In other words, view the other eye to eye, as being an expert in their own area, as being in the same boat and rowing in the same direction—whatever image works. In every conversation, someone may know more about something than the other, but each is an expert in something. The bottom line is that you view them as a peer while in that conversation. Doing so allows you to relax, engage, and be open. By extension, your messaging, body language, and tone will follow, and you are more likely to achieve the buy-in you seek.

Here's a common example I have seen in board meetings. One member might think they're the big kahuna in the meeting. They might be partner at a venture capital firm, with the accompanying money and power, or the board chair with great influence. For whatever reason, they see themselves as holding the most power in the room. However, for effective communication to take place in that meeting, the CEO and that big kahuna must see each other as peers for its duration. Both individuals are there to grow the organization and row in the same direction. The CEO will certainly never get buy-in from this or any board member if they seem unnerved, knocked off their game, or swayed from their vision by anyone in the room. By the same token, if that board member sees the others as less influential or less important individuals who don't have a say, that will be apparent in their presence, tone, and engagement. Throwing one's weight around alienates people and generally does not result in effective conversation. Instead, they will undermine their credibility, the meeting will likely not go well, and turbulence will ensue.

On the other hand, if a leader or board member walks into a meeting perceiving everyone in the room as a peer, their ease, conviction, and demeanor will allow them to secure greater buy-in and wield more influence. Seeing people as equals does not mean that you ignore or disrespect the structural hierarchy, nor does it mean that you have to like them or agree with them or even get along with them. It simply means that for the duration of the conversation, you view them as peers so that your body language, tone, and energy support your message and enable you to communicate effectively and achieve the desired end/get what you need to do your job.

It is common and very human for leaders to view a conversation that involves feedback as something other than peer-to-peer. Whether you're giving positive feedback (which I strongly encourage you to do, as discussed in Chapter 6) or conducting a performance review, think about that conversation as a peer-to-peer dialogue, where the employee is contributing as much as you are, where you are co-creating a solution.

STREAMLINING STRATEGIES

Here are some tools to reframe how you approach conversations with others.

Be Intentional

To be effective in any external dialogue, you have to slow down. Not interested in slowing down? I get it. You have no time. There aren't enough hours in a day. You often jump off one call and onto another, run from one meeting to the next. However, if you don't pause to consider who's on the other side of the conversation, you open yourself up to turbulence.

If you're jumping from email to email to email, and the last one made you angry, take a moment. Don't carry that anger or frustration into the next message. If you don't pause, the text of that next email or call or meeting may sound rushed, harsh, or sharp. Your anger or frustration defines the dialogue, not your actual message.

By taking a few minutes to become intentional about the next conversation, you ensure that your tone, presence, and word choice (and other factors to be discussed in later chapters) are where they need to be for this specific person at this specific time.

Speak Their Language

Imagine how much more effective conversation in a foreign country would be if you spoke the language. Think of how many challenges could be avoided and how much more fun the trip would be.

That's also true in business. Speaking the same language as the person with whom you're communicating can help prevent or at least mitigate misunderstanding and the ensuing turbulence. We often think of language strictly in terms of the vocabulary and syntax used by people in a certain country, but actually, language is more than that. "Language" is the means of human communication that will make the most sense to the person on the other end of your dialogue.

Think about it: the "language" you speak with employees is not the same as the language you speak with your clients. The language you speak with your board of directors is not the same as the language you speak with your C-suite peers. The language you speak with your finance department is not the same language you speak with your marketing department. Before having a conversation with a person or group in your organization, ask yourself, "What language am I speaking? What language does this individual or group of people need to hear?"

Language goes beyond word choice or jargon. Yes, the word *development* means one thing to a fundraiser and something else to an engineer or the Head of Sales, but those individuals also process information, solve problems, and view risk differently. My engineering clients require all the data, research, and backup I can provide. My marketing clients usually want bullet points and easy calls to action. As their leader, it falls on you to speak each language fluently and, on occasion, to serve as translator until they learn to speak the other's language as well.

If you intentionally take a moment before any conversation to ensure that when you walk into that meeting or jump on that call or write that email, you are identifying and speaking the other person's language, you will smooth a lot of bumps in the road.

Leverage the DISC Assessment

Challenges around expectations often result from mismatches in communication style. The DISC assessment is an incredibly useful tool that can help you understand your own communication style. This insight can allow you to leverage your style when it is to your benefit or moderate it when it may not best serve you.[5] A clear understanding of your own DISC profile can also provide some insight into how others engage and communicate. This is helpful when you are looking to speak their language.

Several different DISC assessment reports are available. I use the TTI Success Insights version from Leadership Resources and Consulting for a couple of reasons. First, I find the wording more constructive than others. Second, the structure and layout make it user friendly.

I find two pages related to communication particularly useful for both my clients and myself. The first is titled "How to Communicate with _____ [fill in your name]" and the second is "How Not to Communicate with _____." These pages give my team a roadmap, which provides understanding into how I work and how they can best work with me

---

5   DISC stands for Dominant, Inclusive, Submissive, Compliant and is based on the psychological research of William Moulton Marston.

and vice versa. This assessment is also valuable in working with clients. It provides me with information they might not think to articulate, particularly around how best to engage with them. It also provides them with something to share with their teams.

These pages are especially helpful for communicating with someone you don't know or haven't worked with for very long. They help people understand what will make them successful in having a conversation with you, things that will trigger better outcomes, or words and ways of engaging that will create greater challenges. There is no ideal or "right" profile. Each individual can leverage their own communication style for success. However, understanding yours and that of others is a powerful tool to better speak their language, engage constructively, and avoid triggering turbulence.

Engage in Active Listening

One powerful result of seeing every conversation as a peer-to-peer dialogue is that it opens the door to active listening.

Active listening involves hearing the unspoken messages, the meaning of the silences, and the subtext (the underlying meaning behind the meaning). It is the "conscious processing of the auditory stimuli that have been perceived through hearing."[6] To be good leaders, we must learn to listen actively not just for what is said or omitted but also for what is meant.

Somewhere along the line, not talking became equated with listening, but active listening goes well beyond that. Effective and active listening requires energy, eye contact, and being present.

---

6   Richard West and Lynn H. Turner, *Introducing Communication Theory*, 4th ed. (Boston: McGraw-Hill, 2010).

The *active* part of the listening is how you engage in dialogue even you when you don't say a word.

When we listen actively, we don't just hear verbal responses. Our brain, the world's best computer, also takes in data in the form of tone, convictions, hesitation, clarity, and avoidance. Active listening ensures we don't simply ask the questions we prepared in advance. We ask follow-up questions, pull on threads, and realize there is an underlying situation that may be coloring the conversation.

We have all been in the middle of a conversation and suddenly realize we are mentally getting ready for the next meeting, thinking about the delayed project, or making a grocery list. It happens. But when it does, we can't actively listen at the same time. Call it daydreaming or being distracted, but I call it a conversation killer.

I could write a whole book on active listening, but I don't have to because there are already some great books out there (the Dig Deeper section at the end of the chapter has a few). I encourage everyone to build this muscle. Mastering active listening will help make every conversation more effective and will elevate your leadership.

Don't Delegate or Avoid Conversations

This may seem like an elementary suggestion, but busy leaders commonly delegate conversations or skip them altogether. When we delegate or avoid, we lose the opportunity to connect, listen fully, and engage with clarity. We may unintentionally communicate "I don't have time for you" or "This isn't important to me." Some leaders don't care if that's what they communicate, unfortunately, and that's turbulence waiting to happen. Leaders of rapidly growing companies never have enough time. They are always five steps behind. But prioritizing conversations can be foundational for growth, ultimately sparing you turbulence.

Don't Have the Conversation *for* Them

Finally, be aware of having a conversation with someone else when they don't have the opportunity to actually engage. We have all had a fight with someone in our head. We were mad. We started an argument before ever having a conversation with them, and boy did they give us all the wrong answers. They danced on our last nerve, said everything that makes us angry or reinforces every counterproductive thought we already had. The problem is, they didn't actually say a word. We answered *for* them. We responded the way *we thought* they would respond. But we are not in their head, and we all know the dangers of making assumptions.

The same thing happens in business every day. People talk themselves out of a raise because they have a conversation with their boss in their head and it doesn't go well. Managers avoid engaging with a team member because they assume the person won't take feedback well. Leaders use the insights from focus groups and qualitative surveys but forget to have other conversations. Not having the conversation is as unproductive as putting a new item on a menu without confirming that the chef knows how to make it.

These absent conversations are based solely on assumptions or beliefs, both negative and positive. They happen when we are in a hurry or want to avoid what we imagine to be an uncomfortable conversation. However, it is only fair to let the other person respond for themselves. Chances are, in doing so, you will avoid turbulence or at the least, not make it worse.

TURBULENCE ALERT

I worked with the founder of a growing startup who was making critical decisions about the growth plan of the business, but he was largely having the conversations with himself. When it came to deciding what new market to open next, Brian made assumptions about a particular market without fully engaging his team, getting qualitative feedback from customers, or even conducting broad quantitative surveys. His assumptions led the organization to make a large investment that might not pay off. When I asked why he had chosen the two new markets on his roadmap, he said, "Because we needed to do something." I was speechless. Brian was also creating frustration and concern among the team, who felt the unilateral decision left them and their insights to one side.

I understood Brian's process. He had been quite successful to date and had already scaled and sold another company. In discussing that experience, his first as a sole founder, Brian expressed regret at not trusting his gut more. He felt others had pushed him from his position a bit too often. Although the outcome was successful, he felt opportunities were missed. So now he was committed to making decisions on his own.

First, I convinced Brian to slow down and be more intentional about the decision, simply to see what information might be brought to the table. Next, we made a list of the stakeholders who might have insight or data that should be discussed as part of the expansion conversation. Rather than formal conversations or focus groups, Brian and his team picked up the phone and engaged with people in each group of stakeholders.

By the end of the process, his team felt more engaged and understood the factors in this decision. It also came to light that another market was a better fit and that a strategic partner with whom they were already engaged was interested in helping with the rollout.

SLOW DOWN TO SPEED UP

If your company is growing quickly, it's even more important to ensure that communication is flowing well throughout the organization. As a leader, you need to be aware of how your internal dialogue can undermine or support you. In addition, crafting external dialogues means getting out of your head, taking time to prepare, and thinking of the different audiences you engage with at all different levels of your organization.

The ability to master internal and external dialogue is at the foundation of everything else we cover in this book. It will inform your credibility, how you engage with your team, how authentically you come across, and more. It will also inform your ability to be clear, which is covered next.

TURBULENCE TOOLKIT

To figure out where our challenges lie, we need to slow down. We need to make time to ask ourselves probing questions to find out where we're unknowingly causing or at least allowing turbulence to unsettle our teams. Only then can we start to make a shift and streamline the disruptions. The Turbulence Toolkit at the end of each chapter is designed to help you do just that.

Assess

Each toolkit starts with a list of questions to help you assess where you are today. Your answers will provide insight into what's working or not working and will help you figure out where to start reframing the situation and applying tools to communicate more effectively.

- Is my mindset aligned with my goals?
- Whose voices am I giving a figurative seat at the table?
- Am I giving my own voice a place at the table?
- How is my internal dialogue affecting decision making?
- What facts support my thoughts?
- Have I articulated my thought process to my team, or did I have the conversation for them?
- Do I avoid or delegate conversations based on time or importance of the subject?
- How many important conversations have I delegated in the past month?
- How many important conversations have I skipped in the past month?
- How many conversations in the past month turned out to be more crucial than anticipated?
- Do I block time to prepare for conversations?
- Where do I view the other person on the communication dynamics graphic?
- Did I daydream in that last meeting?

Be Intentional

After you determine where the turbulence lies, you can take steps toward streamlining it and eventually avoiding it altogether. When you're busy, it's common to act on the fly, but you'll decrease the drag and move faster if you slow down first and act intentionally. The statements in this section of each toolkit provide practical strategies to this end.

- Determine the needed mindset first, then work to ensure your internal dialogue aligns.
- Look to support thoughts with facts, not fiction. Write out your counternarratives and then say them out loud.
- In advance of each conversation, give yourself a few minutes to define your intention.
- Keep eye contact in meetings to help you listen actively.
- Beware of talking yourself out of things.
- Beware of when you are getting talked into things.
- Check in with yourself after each conversation to evaluate how it went.

Pick One Thing

No matter how efficient you are, it's impossible to address every disruption at once. After you assess where you are today, pick one thing on which to focus—the one area that would have the biggest impact for yourself and your business if the turbulence were mitigated.

- Conversations with yourself
- Writing down internal dialogue
- Peer-to-peer conversations
- Using the other person's language
- Active listening

Dig Deeper

As stated earlier, it's impossible for any one book to provide an in-depth look at every business challenge. With that in mind, each toolkit ends with resources to help you dig deeper into the challenges causing the most disruption.

- *Active Listening: Improve Your Ability to Listen and Lead* by the Center for Creative Leadership
- *Crucial Conversations: Tools for Talking When Stakes Are High* by Kerry Patterson and Joseph Grenny
- *Leader Effectiveness Training: L.E.T.: Proven Skills for Leading Today's Business into Tomorrow* by Thomas Gordon
- *Radical Candor: Be a Kick-Ass Boss without Losing Your Humanity* by Kim Scott

CHAPTER 2

CLARITY

IT'S YOUR JOB TO BE UNDERSTOOD

"Great leaders are almost always great simplifiers, who can cut through argument, debate, and doubt to offer a solution everybody can understand."

—GENERAL COLIN POWELL

If you've played Pictionary, you've experienced the frustrating challenge when someone on your team can't draw. The person knows what they're supposed to draw, but no matter how hard they try, they can't make it clear to you. They add lines and draw three more dots, then circle one part of the picture over and over, then erase the whole thing and draw it all again, but none of it helps, and your team just keeps guessing and losing.

Regrettably, the equivalent can happen throughout the day in meetings, speeches, and informal conversations. We think that by repeating ourselves or by saying it louder the message will eventually be clear to everyone else because it makes sense to us. Unfortunately, it doesn't work that way.

In Pictionary, the challenges around clarity are twofold: when the picture drawn is not clear to your team, and when the person drawing doesn't understand the clue in the first place. When the latter happens, the person will never be able to draw a picture that's clear to others.

In business, if an idea, vision, or message is not clear to you, you can't make it clear to anyone else. It doesn't matter how much you talk about it, how many different ways you say it, or how much information you throw at it.

Losing a game of Pictionary might cost you a little pride or a bottle of wine if you were feeling ambitious, but it won't cause lasting damage. Lack of clarity in business, however, can create turbulence that affects relationships, timelines, and even the bottom line.

As a leader, it's not other people's job to understand you; it's your job to be understood. If you lack clarity around the company's vision, your value, your expectations, or your boundaries, you won't be able to clearly engage, persuade, inspire, or ultimately lead. In this chapter, we'll talk about the four most common areas where turbulence may result from lack of clarity, as well as suggestions for making things clear.

> "AS A LEADER, IT'S NOT OTHER PEOPLE'S JOB TO UNDERSTAND YOU; IT'S YOUR JOB TO BE UNDERSTOOD."

VISION

Wayne Gretzky famously said, "A good hockey player plays where the puck is. A great hockey player plays where the puck is going to be." A great leader must have a similarly clear vision of where they and the organization are going. Without a clearly articulated vision statement, you can't create a plan for getting there and you certainly can't articulate that plan to motivate and inspire others. As a result, it will be very hard to get people to follow you.

Most people think the company vision is what's at the top of their strategic plan. They spend countless hours and often substantial resources to brainstorm, work, rework, and finalize that statement, but they don't stop to consider if they actually believe it. Vision is not something another person creates for you or that you write on a plan and stick in a drawer. It is the goal—the pot at the end of the rainbow—that should permeate actions and decisions today. For that to happen, the vision must be clear in your own mind first, whether you've taken the time to write it out.

In the Introduction, I wrote about the luxury spa business I founded and successfully grew. It was the biggest thing I had ever created, and I somehow did it without anything more than a vision to build it. But that only took me so far. I couldn't see who we needed to be beyond where we were. Was it a national chain? Was it a franchise opportunity or maybe a boutique business? My internal dialogue provided no clarity. I should have actively sought out conversations, but I didn't. So we plateaued.

In soccer, if there is no goal, players can't score. In business, if there is no vision, growth is hard to sustain. No single book can give you the answer to what *your* clear vision should be, so I've given some resources at the end of this chapter to provide strategies to help you begin to clarify it for yourself.

However, simply having a vision isn't enough. It needs to be both clear to you (see Conversations with Ourselves in Chapter 1) and clearly articulated to everyone else.

BE PRECISE

If you have clear eyesight, you can see things precisely. The edges aren't fuzzy, and you can read both the fine print and the freeway signs with perfect clarity. Ideally, your vision for your company should be just as clear and precise in *all* areas of communication: staff meetings, emails, press releases, one-on-one conversations. Lack of precision, or fuzzy edges, opens the door to miscommunication, misunderstanding, and other forms of turbulence.

In 1975, the founders of Microsoft had a crystal-clear vision: "A computer on every desk in every home in America." Although this statement may not seem quite so visionary today with our laptops and multi-monitor setups, you have to remember that a computer in 1975 was practically the size of a small NYC apartment, the black screen filled with lines of code and blockish letters.

Their statement was bold, and it was also precise. They didn't want to see computers on *most* desks. How many is "most"? Their goal was *every* desk and *every* home. What a clearly articulated vision!

The current CEO of Microsoft, Satya Nadella, has said that this vision had a big flaw because it was a finite goal that the company has achieved. I believe the precise and even finite qualities of the vision are the very reason it worked. Everyone at Microsoft knew what they were building. They knew the hurdles—size, user-friendly interface, cost. They knew, not because someone told them, but because the vision was clear and precise. Everyone could state it. In his book *Microsoft Secrets*, Dave Jaworski called it shared vision.[7]

Today, Microsoft's vision is, "To empower every person and every organization on the planet to achieve more." I'll let you decide if it's precise, and only time will tell if it's effective.

Not every vision has to be as grand as Microsoft's 1975 version, but it should be that clear to everyone, from your clients and bankers to employees and prospects. Clear vision is how you get people on board, motivated and rowing in the same direction.

The realities of rapid growth mean that uncertainty is part of the day-to-day. The 2020 pandemic presented extreme uncertainty; however, general uncertainty around a myriad of shifting factors happens all the time, even if not to the same degree. Circumstances always change. Markets shift, new players arise and change the dynamics—there's always a reason why circumstances or the future might be unclear. For that reason, a clear and articulate vision is crucial. It will help guide you forward through all the external turbulence of the changes around you, helping you keep your sights on where you want to go.

Although clarifying your vision may sound like leadership 101, too often it is viewed as a throwaway. Leaders don't see the value in spending the time to craft and articulate a clear vision. Worse yet, they don't think of the obstacles they may be putting in their own way by not taking that time. As a result, organizations expand, make decisions, and hire with no real sense of where they are going.

---

7   Dave Jaworski, An Insider's View of the Rocket Ride from Worst to First and Lessons Learned on the Journey (New York: Morgan James, 2017).

TURBULENCE ALERT

Recently, I worked with a startup that had already experienced success. They had well-known companies as customers, and they had positive feedback. They were building the tech, adding new features and tools, and bringing on new employees to develop new processes.

These developments were exciting, but they needed resources to grow. However, they attended meeting after meeting with investors and kept hearing things like, "That's interesting" and "Congratulations. You're doing great, but it's not for us."

Finally, they received some meaty feedback: "We just don't know where you're going."

In fact, the founders knew exactly where they were going, but they were having a hard time articulating it to others. The investors couldn't envision where the company was heading, and the only way they could know is if the founders made it clear.

So the CEO and I sat down and began to clarify. We started with the fuzzy generic vision he had been articulating for months: "A platform which helps businesses grow by providing organizational tools using machine learning and an uncluttered interface."

Now, imagine you are an employee. Are you inspired to go to work tomorrow, to build that or sell or market that? Can you even tell me what *that* is? Nonetheless, it was a starting place. We began like an eye doctor would, picking one letter—or in this case, one section—focusing on it and testing it according to two criteria: Is it clear? Is it precise?

I asked the CEO endless questions, starting with, "Are you building a platform or a business? Who wants to tell their clients or friends they built a platform?" I kept pulling on threads, iterating and clarifying, until he finally ended up with, "Seamlessly organized content across organizations on all platforms." The team now knows they have to integrate all types of content (documents, video, audio) across all departments in an organization and on multiple platforms. The customer knows it will be seamless and organized.

This is only a first draft; as the founder clarifies the ultimate destination, his articulation of the vision statement will continue to iterate. However, this version provides enough clarity for investors to "see where they were going," and after months of noes and maybes, the team closed their round within two months.

The CEO's vision hasn't changed, just how it is articulated. As the business grows and the vision becomes clearer, as it surely will, the articulation of the vision will become clearer, too.

In this case, the CEO needed to clarify his vision for an investor meeting, but that is only one example of where it is needed. The vision is articulated in marketing meetings, client meetings, and hiring interviews, and it needs to be clarified in these situations as well. To ensure others are clear on our vision, we need to be precise and concise.

BE CONCISE

For a clearly articulated vision to have its full effect, we need a lot of people to remember it, so keeping it brief has value. I will forever remember my high school English teacher, Mr. Thames, repeatedly saying, "Don't say in five sentences what you can say in one. Don't say in ten words what you can say in five."

"If you can't explain it simply, you don't understand it."

—ALBERT EINSTEIN

We all know the power of Nike's Just Do It campaign. Although it is not their vision statement (which is "to remain the most authentic, connected, and distinctive brand"), Just Do It is clear because it is concise. It is easy to remember and repeat because it is concise.

When working with a client on making a vision statement concise, I like to use what I call the Twitter method, hearkening back to the days when tweets were limited to 140 characters. The exercise forces people to word, reword, and rework their message to keep the vision concise as well as clear.

Can you articulate your vision in 140 characters? Saying more does not necessarily make things clearer. More words, more sentences are simply a sign that we can't state it clearly. The vision statement may end up being a bit more than 140 characters, but this exercise in and of itself helps us clarify.

STREAMLINING STRATEGY

If you're having a hard time getting buy-in from your board of directors, a group of investors, or your own leadership team, unclear vision might be the reason.

Here's a quick test to see how clear your vision is. Have a cross-section of employees in different departments and at different levels quickly record their version of your vision.

Then sit down and listen to or read these statements back-to-back. How clear is your vision? Is it unified across the board? Do the participants see where the organization is going as clearly as you do? Going back to the Pictionary metaphor—do the drawings look the same or at least the same-ish? If people are simply using slightly different words to describe the same vision, that's a sign you're on the right track. However, if the destination is different for every person, then you know your vision isn't clear.

If this is the case, slow down and think through your vision. You might start by being completely honest with yourself: Is your vision truly clear to you? If not, then that is the work. If it is clear to you, then let go of the old vision statement and start with a blank sheet of paper. Sometimes a fresh start is easier than a remodel.

As you go through each person's response, compare it to the clear vision in your mind and then ask yourself a few questions:

- What is clear to each person?
- Is there any point that everyone understood and verbalized?
- What part of the vision are people not repeating back to me?

Your answers to the first two questions will show what is working. The last question will reveal the things you need to revisit: Do you need to find a new way of articulating your vision? Do you need to bring it into new conversations such as onboarding? Do you need to have an all-hands or ask-me-anything meeting? Do the leaders of each department need to talk about vision with their teams during regular reviews? It is through conversation and regular articulation that you can refine and clarify your vision so it can serve you and your team when things get bumpy.

VALUE

Another area where lack of clarity can create turbulence is the value the leader brings to the organization or their role.

We often articulate our value based on the jobs we've done, the tasks we've accomplished, or the skills we've developed. If we've achieved our aims, we feel a strong sense of worth. But working on a task or heading a project does not determine your value; that's in the past. Your value is defined by your present currency *and* what you bring to your future. What you learned, did well, and even got wrong all add to your present and future value. It is not just the experience but the perspective that experience has given you. The experience itself may be personal as well as professional; a combination of the two may be what brings the highest value to the organization.

I have taken a circuitous route to my current business; however, it is not the companies I have led or the tasks I have completed but my experiences and perspectives that make me valuable to my clients.

My first jobs were in theater. I started performing professionally at a young age, became an Equity and SAG actor shortly after graduating from college, and worked in the theater and film industry for the next fifteen years. As a working actor I had to be flexible, take noes in stride, and constantly be ready to show up and promote myself. I had to understand how body language affected an audience's perspective of my character, and I had to quickly and seamlessly adapt to new environments, new coworkers, and a new vision.

Then, at age twenty-four, I co-founded an equity theater company. In this new role, I leveraged the skills that allowed me to confidently walk into any audition with a thick skin and the readiness to hear no. I was able to sit with conviction in front of donors and corporate executives and ask for sponsorship. I never thought of myself as an entrepreneur because that wasn't common terminology in those days. I was an actor who happened to be engaged in this other endeavor.

Later, as the founder of an organization with over a hundred employees, I had to understand customer needs, the power of marketing, and the challenges of hiring and firing, all of which gave me invaluable insight into both the struggles and excitement of building a startup.

These experiences, lessons, and challenges are at the foundation of what I provide my clients and my business. They make me unique. They are my value.

What combination of experiences, skills, and perspectives do you bring to the table? Before you can articulate your value, you have to be clear on what it is. That means slowing down to assess. Although credentials can secure a meeting or open a door, your value goes far beyond degrees and titles. It is a combination of wins and losses, tools and strategies, self-awareness, and development that make up your value.

You may wonder how clarifying your value can support rapid growth. A clear sense of value enables you to motivate employees, close sales, and create buy-in, all of which streamlines turbulence so growth is not slowed. Clarifying your value for yourself allows you to articulate it in a precise, meaningful way to those around you—your clients, your manager, your board of directors, and your team. Clarifying and leaning into your value also helps you know whom to hire to add strength and diversity to your team. This allows you to spend your day working in your highest value—in that which brings the greatest return to your project or company—and allows those you hire to do the same, leading to a more productive team and business.

As one of my clients learned, clarifying your value can also lead to new, previously unconsidered career opportunities (see the In Their Own Words sidebar). Even if you're simply looking to change jobs within the same company, you might be short-changing yourself because you haven't taken the time to assess and articulate your true value.

Knowing your highest value ensures you're in the right position, getting the right promotion, walking the path to success that's right for you. Knowing your highest value also helps reinforce the credibility and influence you have as a leader in your organization. Sometimes leveraging your highest value is simply about elevating yourself and constantly reinforcing your own credibility and influence.

IN THEIR OWN WORDS: KATHLEEN

Kathleen is a former client who spent fifteen years in corporate events. She was successful and well respected, but she hated her job and she didn't know what else she wanted to do or how to figure it out. The process involved clarifying both her vision and her value, which she explains here in her own words:

> There was never a specific moment when a light went off. I had been feeling I was in the wrong role for years. I'm not sure that it occurred to me that I could go to a different industry. I wasn't sure how to move my skills over into something different. I only knew I wasn't in the right place.
>
> I did know that I wanted to work somewhere where the hard work that I put in was recognized, where I felt that

my voice was heard. I wanted to feel like I was growing in my career and that I wasn't just stuck in one spot.

During one of our meetings, I threw out a question that Kathleen had not considered: "What if you just didn't work there?" Thinking back on the moment during our interview, she said,

> I felt like a weight was lifted off my shoulders, and I thought, "Yeah, what if I didn't work there? I could support myself until I found the right thing." I felt like that could open up the space for figuring out what I actually wanted to do, instead of just feeling like I want to do something different.
>
> Emergency management has always been something that interests me. I wish I had studied it in undergrad. Once I gave myself the space [to consider a career in this field], I was so excited to tell everyone what I wanted to be doing. I no longer felt unsure. I knew exactly what skills to promote and how to communicate them. With this clarity, I became my own biggest advocate and spokeswoman.
>
> So I began looking at job postings, and a position for an emergency management program manager popped up. As I read the description, I thought, "I can do that and that and that."
>
> Around that time, I had been out with some friends and our boat broke down, and it wasn't a great situation. I grew up sailing, so jumped into action and said, "Okay, this is what we're going to do. And these are the steps we're going to take."
>
> I thought about that experience as I read the job posting and thought, "You know what? I can do this."
>
> At that point, a path started to become clear. I started to understand how I was going to get there. I had always been self-aware enough to know my strengths.

However, I didn't know how to translate them in the right language for a new industry. Now I knew that I had the skills in my toolbox because I had already taken the time to list them. Event planning became project management. Guest check-in became database administration.

All of this made me better able to articulate my value. I also had a lot more confidence because I was no longer wandering around, looking for a direction. I knew which path I was on and where I needed to make turns, so I was able to say to people, "I am going this way. Do you have any suggestions for a better route to get there?" As a result, people I didn't know said to me, "Your passion for this shines through, and I'm really inspired by your motivation."

Once I applied for the program manager position, things moved quickly. In the interview, I was able to answer really pointed questions like "What steps did you take to get here?" and "How do you think what you have done will translate in this role?" I could confidently say, "Here's an example of a time when I did this, and these were the results that came from it. And I see that applying to this role in X, Y, Z way."

During the second interview, they said, "You answered all the interview questions. We're really just trying to get a feel for who you are." I thought, "Okay, I know that I did a good job articulating my value and what I can bring to this team. Since they called me back for a second interview, they clearly see some of that." At that point, I felt like it was less of an interview and more of a conversation, so I asked myself, "Do I want to work with them? Do I want to be a part of this team?"

I also felt that if I didn't want this job, then I didn't have to accept it. Confidence was a huge aspect of being able to say that. Having clarity on not just what I wanted to do but also the type of work environment and the type of relationship with my boss I wanted helped me find just that. Everything I wrote down to describe what I knew I was looking for is what I found.

When we touched base for this interview, Kathleen had been in her new role at FEMA for six months. In that time, her boss nominated her for the Special Act Award, which she received. To her, it was a bonus and some recognition for the work she'd been doing. She says it validated that she was clearly in the right place.

EXPECTATIONS

During a panel discussion at South by Southwest, one participant made a remark that has stuck with me for years: "Don't bring me a Monday problem on a Friday." In other words, you can bring me your problems, but don't dump something on me Friday afternoon and expect me to solve it for you over the weekend. Talk about crystal-clear expectations! By stating this up front, this leader averted potential turbulence on two fronts: for the team, who might not get what they need in time if they came to her on Friday, and for the leader, because the lack of forethought would likely piss her off.

Lack of clarity around expectations can cause disruptions at many levels. Whether it's the expectations set for new hires during onboarding or something as simple as deadlines, clarity around expectations ensures everyone is on the same page.

In rapidly growing organizations, needs are constantly changing, which means expectations are constantly changing. Yet many leaders don't take time to slow down and articulate those expectations. If expectations shift, leaders may forget to go back and clarify that fact. Even if they do articulate expectations, leaders often don't ensure the other person understands them.

Expectations will be discussed further in relation to onboarding (Chapter 5) and conflict (Chapter 7). For now, remember this: as a leader, part of your job is to ensure expectations are clear, precise, and articulated in a way that people understand.

UNCLEAR EXPECTATIONS

According to a Gallup report titled *State of the American Workplace*, unclear and misaligned expectations are the number one reason for demotivated employees. Only one in ten said they know what is expected of them.[8] As leaders, the onus is on us to set clear expectations. However, too often we assume or outline but do not clearly articulate what we expect. I realize rapid growth means you are busy and that taking the time to ensure expectations are clear is not at the top your to-do list. But effective leaders always find time, even if it's only fifteen minutes, because danger lies ahead if you don't.

I find the breakdown in expectations happens in one of four ways:

1. You don't actually think you need to state them.
2. You thought you stated them but didn't.
3. You stated them, but they weren't understood.
4. You stated them, but they were inconsistently communicated from employee to employee.

Any of these four situations opens the door to unmet expectations, frustrations, and friction—that is, turbulence. There is a reason we set deadlines. They are clear, and we know when something is due. When we see store signs that read "No shoes,

---

8   Gallup, State of the American Workplace, 2017, https://www.gallup.com/workplace/238085/state-american-workplace-report-2017.aspx.

no shirt, no service," we are clear about what is expected of us. Why should other expectations be any different?

TURBULENCE ALERT

A client of mine, Elizabeth, had to craft and deliver a very complex and multifaceted presentation to a prestigious and influential group that would have a say in her organization's growth. Her team was given a full day for the presentation. Honestly, it could have gone on for days, there was so much detail and nuance, but who wants to sit through that presentation?

Early on in the process, we realized much of the content and terminology could be open to different interpretations. So in the introductory section we outlined expectations.

Elizabeth let the audience know that each presenter would speak for fifteen minutes and then open up the conversation for Q&A. This set the expectation that each section wouldn't be long and that they should hold their questions, which helped avoid interruptions. She also defined some key terms that were unique to her organization or that could be misconstrued. The definitions helped the attendees know what to expect as the stories unfolded.

Lack of clear expectations can lead to missed deadlines, conflict on teams, disruptions on projects, or employees blindsided by a firing because they didn't know they were not meeting expectations.

Here's how my former client Kathleen used expectation setting to streamline some turbulence with a colleague:

I worked on a hiring assessment project, which is a big undertaking for our department and something that a colleague had been working on. Once I started in my new role, he started to push more and more of it toward me. He, however, was no longer really participating. I felt like he had pushed much of his responsibility off onto me, possibly because he simply didn't want to do it. So we had a conversation where I said, "Ben, do you need me to take this off your plate and lead it? Or are you looking for support? Because if you're looking for support, then I need clear direction from you of where we're going. But if you want me to lead it, then I will do that. And I will explain to you what I need in terms of support."

He thought about it for a minute, then said, "I really need to focus on this other thing. Would you mind taking this and running with it?" After that, I didn't feel like he was dumping his work on me because now it was my work, and I could do it my way and still get what I needed from him. And he didn't feel like I was taking his project from him because we had had this conversation.

TURBULENCE ALERT

One of my clients was a Chief Compliance Officer. When given data to analyze, Maria required uninterrupted quiet time to work in a productive and focused way. Fortunately, she had a private office, with a door. Unfortunately, she never closed her door, concerned that she would seem unwelcoming. By keeping her door open, she set the expectation that she was always available. People felt comfortable talking to her and they valued her opinion, so they popped in and out of her office all day, making it difficult for her to concentrate. She ended up staying late almost daily so she could focus without interruptions once everyone had left.

Maria had to figure out a way to leverage her role as a trusted, go-to person for bouncing ideas around and seeking insight—an important role that made her valuable to the organization—without undermining her focus and work. We found a simple solution: she started closing her office door when she really needed to focus. She found this challenging because she didn't want to communicate to others that she was off limits or that she wasn't accessible. The answer: whenever she needed to close the door to focus, Maria put a Post-it note on the door that said, "I'm in the weeds. Back at 3." Doing so set an expectation that she would be back, and it provided a precise time. This allowed her to feel comfortable closing the door to do the work because people knew they could come back later. Within two weeks, her stress level decreased. She didn't have to stay late, and she became increasingly comfortable closing her door.

STREAMLINING STRATEGIES

Much like being precise when articulating your vision or your value, being precise when articulating expectations helps ensure everyone is on the same page. Here are a few practical tools for expectations that you can put in place right now.

VERBALIZE AVAILABILITY

We all have internal deadlines related to tasks we need to accomplish, but we don't think of those tasks as being part of expectation setting. Saying something like, "Yes, I can meet with you, but not until after 1:00 p.m." allows us to be on the same page with other people and still meet those internal deadlines.

Set Office Hours

Another useful tool, especially in virtual settings, is setting office hours, whether it's the same time every morning or certain times throughout the week, so that you ensure you are not otherwise occupied and are fully available. You set expectations by communicating, "You can expect me to be available and fully present between nine and eleven on Tuesday morning." If they reach out at eleven thirty, you will have moved on to something else.

Articulate Response Times

You can also clarify expectations around email responses. You may be too busy to fully respond to an email today, but you can let the person know you received their message and that you will respond by the end of business the next day. Set a clear, precise, meaningful expectation so the person doesn't wait for a response or assume you are ignoring them. This also helps prevent a second questioning email. It's not enough to think about expectations; you have to clearly, precisely articulate them verbally or in writing.

BOUNDARIES

Expectations are always evolving; they're iterative. Boundaries, on the other hand, are lines that shouldn't be crossed. They are set in stone in a way that expectations usually aren't. When a business hangs its hours on a sign, that's a boundary, not an expectation. When you walk into a Starbucks, you can expect to find comfy sofas; that's an expectation, not a boundary.

Whatever your role in an organization, there are boundaries—some set for you and some you have to set for yourself. The lack of clearly set and articulated boundaries creates many types of turbulence. It can show up when a CEO repeatedly allows a certain influential board member to use up too much oxygen during meetings, when a leader allows one squeaky wheel on the team to get all the grease, or when a bullying coworker intimidates to get their way.

As a good Texas girl, I like to imagine boundaries as fences on a ranch. If your neighbor's property has a bunch of cattle and you don't have a fence on your land, at some point that cattle will mosey over to your land and start grazing. Although that may not be a problem in the short term, over time that may create a scarcity of resources for your own cattle. The neighbor's cattle aren't intentionally or maliciously eating all of your grass. They're doing it because there are no boundaries. There's no fence to show them when they are crossing the line.

If you put up a fence after cattle have already been grazing on your land, they are likely to push hard against that boundary because they're used to walking right over that line. Your job is not only to put up the fence but also to continually fortify the fence to make sure it holds. Eventually, the cattle will realize there is a clear line that they cannot cross.

The same is true with professional boundaries. We have to set clear lines for ourselves and others. Setting clear boundaries is not a point of aggression or defensiveness. It is simply a way of communicating "This is the line that cannot be crossed." Like a rancher who sets up a new fence, you have to continually articulate and reinforce your boundaries because people will push up against the fence, especially if they are in the habit of crossing the line. You are asking for behaviors to change. However, the minute you let one person cross over, you are communicating to others that they can cross that boundary, too. Letting somebody get away with crossing the line diminishes and undermines your own credibility.

TURBULENCE ALERT

I worked with the CEO of a late-stage startup that had done incredibly well. A new, big player had come into the market, so Jack had to make big shifts to stay ahead. He had one board member who was always swimming against the current, pushing against his decisions and leadership. Jack knew this board member would replace him if he had the votes.

Ahead of one board meeting, Jack prepared his plan for the next fiscal year, including how the company would meet the challenge presented by the new player. Thinking ahead to his presentation, Jack assumed (internal dialogue) the board member would resist his recommendations. If he would have walked into the meeting with that defensive posture, Jack would have undermined his own stature as CEO.

We discussed how he could set a boundary in advance so he didn't feel the need to defend his position during the meeting. Jack reached out to the individual ahead of time and said, "I know your thoughts on this plan, and I realize it's not a plan on which we are in agreement. When I present it during the board meeting, I will take the first thirty minutes to lay out the plan in full and then open it up for discussion." In this way, Jack set a boundary that gave him enough breathing room to get through his narrative and prevent this individual from jumping on him at the beginning. This allowed Jack to find his groove and present the plan without feeling like he needed to defend himself or his proposal.

What boundaries do you set within your leadership team? What boundaries do you set for your employees? What boundaries do you set for your clients? Some companies may believe the "customer is always right," but others may choose to set limits, requiring certain levels of respect or consistency. If you're the leader of an organization, make sure your boundary lines are clear, not only to customers but also to employees who will be helping you reinforce them. You can't be at every square inch of that fence all day, every day.

Sometimes people have boundaries in mind but don't articulate them because they don't want to be seen as defensive or even aggressive. The reality is that boundaries, like fences, are not judgmental. They are not mean or confrontational. They are simply a framework that allows businesses to run smoothly and leaders to own their space. Being seen as aggressive in setting those boundaries has more to do with how you state them than the boundaries themselves (more on tone and word choice in Chapter 3).

Boundaries often show up in personal dynamics as well. There will always be people who seek to leverage their position or power to dominate or intimidate. They may want something done their way, or they may feel the need to micromanage. Some even leverage power simply because they believe they can. With these individuals, setting clear boundaries from the beginning is especially important. We cannot start clarifying a poorly or inadequately articulated boundary in the middle of a conversation; it needs to be clear from the beginning. We cannot control how others respond, but we can own and hold our boundaries.

TURBULENCE ALERT

I always invite my clients to reach out if they need me, even if it is between sessions. This began as an open invitation, until one client slowly—almost imperceptibly—started inching up to and crossing over the line. He began emailing more often, then calling more often, and then wanting email responses late at night or answered calls at two o'clock on a Sunday afternoon.

At some point I realized that I had allowed this person to creep over the line to the point where he was both encroaching on my time for other clients and getting more of my value than he was paying for according to our original agreement. I started to feel frustrated and, frankly, exhausted by his demands.

I also realized he had crossed a line that in my mind was very clear but obviously wasn't clear to him. I knew that with future clients, I needed to be more precise about this boundary, so I wrote a new clause into every client agreement, stating that I am available between 8:00 a.m. and 5:00 p.m., Monday through Friday. In doing so, I let clients know when I am available and also when I'm not: if they reach out after 5:00 p.m. or on the weekends, I won't respond until Monday after 8:00 a.m.

At first, I put off having a conversation with this individual. He was a great client who had given me several referrals, and he had achieved some of his original goals. Finally, I had to be clear and take my own advice, no matter how uncomfortable. I told him, "I'm finding that our original engagement isn't robust enough for what you need. I'd love to offer you another option that might give you more of the support you're looking for."

As soon as I presented it that way and put something in writing, he realized how regularly he'd been reaching out. Ultimately, he decided to move up to a deeper engagement. He got the support he needed, and I was able to maintain my boundaries.

WORD CHOICE

In each of these buckets around clarity—whether you're articulating vision, value, expectations, or boundaries—it is important to be precise, and the best way to do that is through your word choice.

When my son was eleven, he was told in a parent-teacher conference to be "less silly," but he was given no explanation as to what exactly that meant. Did he need to sit still? Chat less? Not giggle? The lack of clarity meant my son didn't know how to act to meet the teacher's expectations, and I didn't know how to support him. This imprecise expectation set him up for failure and led to frustration for both of us.

I believe in keeping superlatives and meaningless prefixes out of conversation. Telling an investor that you've been "super successful" is meaningless. How you define "successful"—or "super," for that matter—might be quite different from the investor's definition. Instead, pick precise words: "We've increased sales by 25 percent quarter over quarter."

Since speaking their language is important, consider your audience when choosing your words. Are you talking to investors who want to hear a financial conversation? Are you talking to employees who want to hear an inspirational version of your vision? Are you a scientist talking to a group of scientists who share your language, or are you talking to a room of laymen? Knowing the audience will help you pick the most precise words for your listeners, enabling you to communicate the exact message you want them to hear.

TURBULENCE ALERT

James is an outspoken leader who is trying to effect meaningful change at a time of crisis in his organization, but he has unintentionally turned into a boat rocker on his leadership team. His natural way of engaging can come across as confrontational, and it's not serving him well in this situation.

Before he sent a letter to a fellow member of the board on which he served, James let me read it. The original letter said, "We have the opportunity to *change* the situation." *Change* is a tough word. Some people love change, but most people don't. Asking your team to change (or yourself, for that matter) can make them uncomfortable and worried. Change can be scary and hard because it requires a journey into the unknown. So we replaced the word *change* so that the sentence read, "We have the opportunity to *stabilize* the situation."

By adjusting that one word, we made James's intention more precise. The word *change* doesn't necessarily mean the situation will improve, whereas *stabilize* gives the sense that a certain amount of chaos will be leveled off. It was a simple way of making the message more precise and avoiding the implied stress of change.

The hard part in choosing the best word to paint the right picture is taking the time to do so. I keep a thesaurus open on a daily basis. However, one word can mean the difference in securing buy-in, making a sale, or inspiring your team.

SLOW DOWN TO SPEED UP

As you can see, the need for clarity is everywhere in your organization. You may wonder, however, what clarity has to do with rapid growth. I leave you with this: how fast can you drive in heavy fog? Clarity is key if you want your people to be able to drive forward with confidence, speed, and efficacy.

In the next chapter, we'll consider the nonverbal elements of communication, how they inform executive presence, and how they can enhance or undermine your credibility as a leader.

TURBULENCE TOOLKIT

Assess

- How precise is the vision statement on our website?
- Is the team aligned on the vision?
- Are clients clear on our value prop?
- Do others see and reflect back to me my value?
- Am I finding it challenging to engage and inspire investors?
- Does my sales pitch say in five sentences what I could convey in one?
- First thing this morning, could I have clearly articulated my biggest objective for the day?
- Can I concisely explain to a friend why I was hired for my position?
- Did my team ask why when I told them about a critical decision?
- Do I feel a certain coworker, boss, or board member is challenging a boundary?
- Does my team fall short of expectations?
- Are deadlines regularly met?

Be Intentional

- Be honest with yourself about how clear you are on your idea, your decision, or your vision.

- As an alternative to recording responses, give each employee or team member a multiple-choice quiz and ask them to pick out the organization's vision.
- Before the big meeting or sales conversation, take the time to be clear on what you need to say.
- Get on the same page with others by writing out mutual expectations. It can be in a document before a meeting or in a follow-up email.
- Define your boundaries before you need them. It is hard, if not impossible, once someone is grazing on your land.
- Rearticulate boundaries often and without judgment.
- Love your thesaurus. The right words can make all the difference.

Pick One Thing

- Clarifying your vision
- Articulating your value
- Setting expectations
- Holding boundaries
- Prioritizing word choice

Dig Deeper

- *Leading through Language: Choosing Words That Influence and Inspire* by Bart Egnal
- *Made to Stick: Why Some Ideas Survive and Others Die (Principle 1)* by Chip Heath and Dan Heath
- *Microsoft Secrets: An Insider's View of the Rocket Ride from Worst to First and Lessons Learned on the Journey* by Dave Jaworski
- *Start with Why: How Great Leaders Inspire Everyone to Take Action* by Simon Sinek
- *Vivid Vision: A Remarkable Tool for Aligning Your Business around a Shared Vision of the Future* by Cameron Herold
- *Words Can Change Your Brain: 12 Conversation Strategies to Build Trust, Resolve Conflict, and Increase Intimacy* by Andrew Newberg and Mark Robert Waldman

CHAPTER 3

CREDIBILITY

PERCEPTION IS REALITY

"You go to the White House, you shake hands with [Teddy] Roosevelt and hear him talk, and then you go home and wring the personality out of your clothes."

—RICHARD WASHBURN CHILD

If you have ever watched an episode of *Law & Order*, you have probably noticed what happens when defendants go to trial: they put on a new suit or dress, shave and comb their hair, and generally present themselves as buttoned-up and respectable as possible. Lawyers also work with defendants and witnesses to prepare their testimony. They discuss eye contact, posture, and tone of voice while on the witness stand. The goal is to boost their credibility to help support the attorney's narrative to the jury.

As a leader, you too can elevate your credibility—or you can undermine it—with messages you communicate but never say outright, perceived in your level of confidence, your tone of voice, your body language, and your energy. Credibility is at the heart of how a leader wants to be perceived. Unfortunately, as leaders move up the ladder, many don't think about how their presence affects their credibility; they also fail to consider how their presence needs to evolve as their organization and role grow. Rapid growth in particular leaves little time to evaluate and iterate on something that, to their mind, doesn't lead to a bigger bottom line. The truth is that credibility is central to a leader's success in motivating their team, persuading customers, and broadening their influence, all of which—along with presence—impact productivity, employee engagement, and other factors that ultimately do affect the financial success of the company.

Credibility is defined as "the quality or power of inspiring trust." Trust is defined as "assured reliance on the character, ability, strength, or truth of someone or something." No one will follow a leader they don't trust. Credibility, confidence, and presence go hand in hand because collectively, they inspire trust. If the way you show up does not align with what you say, what you do, or who you claim to be, your presence will be undermined and you will fail to engender trust. In 2017, Edelman released their Trust Barometer Report, which showed that CEO credibility was at 37 percent, an all-time low, and by extension, trust was equally diminished.[9] A lack of credibility directly impacts trust.

A study of 268 senior executives by Coqual (formerly the Center for Talent Innovation) said executive presence counts for 26 percent of what it takes to get promoted.[10] That is almost a

---

9   "2017 Edelman Trust Barometer," Edelman, January 21, 2017, www.edelman.com/trust/2017-trust-barometer.

10   Sylvia Ann Hewlett, Lauren Leader-Chivée, Laura Sherbin, and Joanne Gordon, with Fabiola Dieudonné, "Executive Presence," Coqual, formerly Center for Talent Innovation, 2013, https://coqual.org/wp-content/uploads/2020/09/26_executivepresence_keyfindings-1.pdf.

third. But how often in your busy workday do you ensure you are showing up with all stakeholders in a way that supports both you and your business?

In this chapter, we'll look at the facets of credibility, the role confidence plays in strengthening your presence, and how you can shift perception to the reality you want.

CONFIDENCE

Confidence plays a critical part in how credibly a leader is perceived and, by extension, trusted. In fact, confidence is such a powerful tool that the word is used to describe a certain type of person: a confidence man, or con man. With con artists—who are gifted in getting others to trust them, even when they should not—the reality ultimately undermines the perception, but for leaders, the power of confidence is foundational to their credibility.

In my ten years of working with leaders, I have come to realize that to build credibility and influence, leaders need to address the two sides of confidence: *belief*, which refers to the confidence you have in yourself, and *presence*, which relates to the confidence others have in you. One is internal: a belief or mindset (covered in Chapter 1). The other external: your executive presence (covered in the next section of this chapter).

To help my clients understand the theory behind my model and to help them begin to identify where they can focus their efforts to effect constructive growth, I created the Confidence Matrix in Figure 3.1.

CONFIDENCE MATRIX

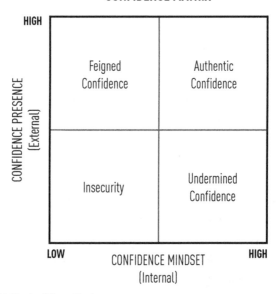

Figure 3.1. The Confidence Matrix

The horizontal axis is the internal confidence or mindset, which relates to our beliefs. The vertical axis is the external confidence or presence—how we are perceived by others. Both axes go from low to high. We are all some combination of low to high external and low to high internal confidence, which manifests in one of the four quadrants.

The quadrant we fit into may change as we move into different roles, organizations, or even situations. However, over the course of the day, month, or year, we are likely to play most comfortably in one quadrant more than others. The goal is to strive to be in the upper right quadrant of Authentic Confidence, where you maintain a strong belief of your value and exude a confident external presence to others. Authentic Confidence is where leaders do their best work, establish and maintain the most trust, and create the greatest impact for their organizations and themselves.

I like to bring the matrix to life and illustrate how each quadrant manifests itself, so I assign each quadrant a fictional character. However, I bet you can fill each quadrant with leaders you know, have worked with, or admire.

Here are the ones I currently use in my work.

Lower Left: Insecurity. Here, I put in Ann Perkins from *Parks and Recreation.* Ann is unsure of herself internally, and it shows up in the way she often makes herself small and bites her lip. She is memorable but not viewed as a leader like the series' protagonist, Leslie Knope. She does have great influence with Leslie, but most people don't see it. Her insecure presence makes her an ineffectual character on the show.

You may find it challenging to find a leader you admire who fits into this box, which serves to illustrate the point: insecure leaders are generally not recognized or promoted.

Upper Left: Feigned Confidence. Regional Manager Michael Scott from *The Office* tries to come across as puffed up and on top of things. He takes up space, attempts to command a room, and uses his voice to establish authority. However, when Michael talks directly to the camera, we can see that he is often unsure, almost trying to convince himself of his own authority. The effect is that others often view him as bumbling and hard to respect.

Lower Right: Undermined Confidence. Harry Potter, protagonist of J. K. Rowling's bestselling series about a boy wizard, knows he has magical powers. Even in the first book, when he is first discovering who he is and what he can do, Harry believes in his abilities. But he is not viewed by others as a leader. The insults he receives from jealous peers and his mean-spirited relatives undermines his own confidence, making him tentative, with a small presence. This changes over time as his confidence grows and others see that reflected in his presence.

Upper Right: Authentic Confidence. Here, I use James Bond—the Bond of your choice will do. I could get into the Connery versus Craig debate, but even if you choose Pierce Brosnan or Roger Moore, each Bond actor created a character with a high belief in their own value, whose external presence inspires trust in one and all. Even Bond's nemeses don't underestimate him. His presence and mindset align. The result is a credible and trusted leader. His body language, tone, and energy perfectly match his confident mindset. They are also perfectly suited to his role.

You may wonder how this matrix is relevant for an already successful leader of a rapidly growing organization. First, you can use this matrix tool when looking to develop your team and build a strong bench in your organization. If you know someone who has high belief in their value but their external presence doesn't align (Undermined Confidence), you can help them elevate their executive presence through shifts in tone, word choice, and body language. If you realize someone may look the part but their word choices or tone belie their confidence and presence (Feigned Confidence), helping them understand their mindset may be the place to start.

Second, even successful leaders experience moments that may cause them to question themselves or receive hard questions from others—perhaps when they're pushed into new terrain or facing new challenges (pandemic, anyone?). It is just as fundamental to assess how we are making our way through these challenges as it is to review data and analytics when developing a new product; you can complete that assessment using this matrix. We need to iterate to improve.

Your internal belief in your value can be strengthened by mastering internal dialogue, learning new skills, reaching out to a mentor, or hiring a leadership coach; these strategies can build on the mindset strategies we already covered in Chapter 1. However, internal confidence is only one half of the coin. As a leader, it's important to make sure your external confidence or executive presence is aligned with your abilities, belief, and role. This is key to getting people to trust and follow you.

PRESENCE

Executive or leadership presence is sometimes defined as the ability to portray confidence and gravitas as a leader. That is the goal. Others form opinions of us as soon as we enter a room or show up on their screens. Many people take the time to thoughtfully consider their professional attire to "dress the part," but they fail to consider how their presence informs their message, role, or organization. Presence is not just about how you dress, although attire does play a role in informing others' perceptions. If you only dress the part but all your nonverbal signals undermine you, you will simply be an empty suit.

We all know the adage about not getting a second chance to make a first impression. We also know we all have blind spots. As a leader, these blind spots can undermine you and, by extension, the organization as a whole—especially blind spots you choose not to see or, worse, see and choose not to address. There's no way to avoid turbulence for the broader group if you're undermined as a leader by your own ineffectual presence.

Let's break down the elements of presence and discuss how they inform the way we are perceived, as well as how to become more intentional about building a presence that supports our organizations.

ASPECTS OF PRESENCE

In 1967, Albert Mehrabian released his research on how non-verbal cues and behaviors impact interpersonal exchange. You may have heard about the 7 percent, 38 percent, 55 percent rule: Mehrabian's research showed that how we are perceived is 7 percent *verbal* (what we say), 38 percent *vocal* (how we say it), and 55 percent *visual* (what our body communicates).[11]

Over the years, people have criticized these findings, but it is important to remember that the research focused on decoding inconsistent communication. This goes back to the need to ensure that how we show up aligns with what we say, what we do, and who we claim to be. My classical theatrical training and ten years working with business leaders have made it clear that this verbal-vocal-visual formula is likely true. We covered the verbal aspect in the chapter on clarity. In this chapter, we'll discuss the vocal and visual facets, along with a fourth element I refer to as energy.

Vocal (Tone)

Whereas the verbal facet involves the actual words you say, vocal—that is, tone—describes how you say it. The vocal aspect of presence is often overlooked, but the way we say things communicates a great deal. Frustration shows up in tone. Excitement shows up in tone. Urgency shows up in tone.

---

11 The World of Work Project, "Mehrabian's 7-38-55 Communication Model: It's More Than Words," World of Work Project, n.d., https://worldofwork.io/2019/07/mehrabians-7-38-55-communication-model/; A. Mehrabian and M. Wiener, "Decoding of Inconsistent Communications." Journal of Personality and Social Psychology 6 (1967): 109–114.

Tone is complex and multilayered. It involves pitch, pace, volume, and inflection. Words like *curt*, *rushed*, or *pissed* are communicated largely in tone rather than message. People use the full crayon box of tone every day. For example, the "baby talk" used with children or pets has more to do with tone than the actual words spoken.

"We often refuse to accept an idea merely because the tone of voice in which it has been expressed is unsympathetic to us."

—FRIEDRICH NIETZSCHE

Despite the power of tone, we often fail to leverage it to our advantage in establishing a credible presence. In business, for some reason, we stumble into meetings and conversations without slowing down to check our tone, which can be affected by mood, mindset, and culture.

Let's start with culture. I grew up in a Spanish household. Conversations at large family meals were passionate, assured, and determined—at least, that's how we might describe them. To non-Spanish outsiders, our conversations might have sounded loud, brash, and aggressive.

Years ago, I visited my family in Spain with my very British boyfriend. He didn't speak any Spanish and would sit listening, not to *what* we were saying but to our tone. After a few days, he was able to articulate the tone often heard in Spain: "Everything sounds so accusatory." I was surprised by his assessment; no one in Spain intends to sound that way. Spaniards are usually very welcoming and friendly folks who generally love life. However, to those from different cultures who are used to speaking with a different tone—both literally and figuratively—the message can come across as blunt, brash, and apparently, accusatory.

Although Spaniards come across as loud, people from other cultures may come across as soft-spoken or even lyrical. In our global world, clients, investors, and employees may cross multiple cultures. As leaders, we must be aware of how our tone may help or hurt us.

TURBULENCE ALERT

I worked with a client who, although very bright, communicated with what can only be described as an angry tone. Mark was not an angry person. However, his natural New York style came across as unreserved and forceful in his messaging. We started working together because he had a heavy lift at his organization that required some nimble persuasion. He did not see that his tone might create issues with some stakeholders. His boss, however, did.

As we began working together, I saw Mark was direct and strong—admirable, often necessary traits, but they can also create turbulence in some situations. I traveled to visit him onsite at a stakeholder meeting. I wanted to see how he was showing up with this key constituency. It didn't take long for me to hear what others had been hearing. His direct and strong vocal presence sounded like rapid machine-gun fire. Mark moved from question to question with curt, forceful, and missile-like responses. His tone completely undermined his credibility. The meeting devolved into an angry back-and-forth, with some people getting up and leaving. No persuasion was achieved that day.

Although much of this tone had to do with Mark's natural style, that natural style became an obstacle, especially as his impatience increased with the urgent need to secure buy-in. Here, the key was to find ways for Mark to communicate as directly but with the force of a Nerf gun instead of an Uzi.

Our mood or mindset also plays a significant role in our tone. In a staff meeting, your tone will be different when you are sharing good news versus bad, and rightly so. However, if you know bad news that you can't yet share, that distraction or disappointment will affect your tone, and the knock-on effect might be that your team thinks you're unfocused, abrupt, or stressed. Even if you want to delay sharing the bad news, with your tone, you've already communicated that something's not quite right.

Tactics for shifting your tone vary widely, depending on the person, the situation, and the needed shift. In Mark's case, for example, his intense, machine gun style came out in short blunt sentences delivered loudly and rapidly. Shifting his tone to something less intense might involve lowering the volume a bit and speaking more slowly.

On the other end of the spectrum, someone might be so soft-spoken that their direct comments don't have the needed impact, like a Nerf bullet flopping onto the floor instead of hitting its target. This person might need to add a little force to their words and work on breath support.

Addressing turbulence caused by tone is specific and individual. For help in determining the tone that's causing disruptions and for strategies in making a shift, check out the resources in the Dig Deeper sections, specifically *Executive Presence: The Art of Commanding Respect Like a CEO* by Harrison Monarth or *The Power of Presence: What Actors Can Teach Business Leaders* by Christopher Von Baeyer. Additional tools are provided in the Streamlining Strategies section.

Rapidly growing companies or teams are particularly at risk for turbulence created by tone. Fast-moving environments radiate urgency, complexity, and stress, which can affect our tone and, by extension, how we show up.

Ensuring your vocal quality matches your verbal and your visual is key to establishing your credibility. A disconnect between them can be perceived as inauthentic and false. For example, a person who speaks like the stereotypical used car salesman or infomercial host would have much less success as a doctor or trial attorney. Creating the right pace and pitch for your overall presence and even for each varying situation is a matter of practice. If you are a doctor giving complicated news to a patient, you may want to slow down to keep from overwhelming them. By the same token, I always need to speed up when I'm working with what I affectionately call a pants-on-fire organization (no judgment there; it's just the way they work).

Inflection is easy to control but hard to hear in your own voice. We never think our voice is flat and monotonous, yet we have all met people like that, as well as "over-inflectors," who end up sounding as if they are singing while speaking. Inflection gives color, variety, and emphasis to our words. Singers and actors often mark their scripts to remind them where to prioritize a word or thought. You can do the same. Go through your one-on-one conversation, speech, pitch, or presentation and ensure that your inflection highlights your subtext, not just your text. Again, the Dig Deeper section has resources to help you dive deep into this process.

TURBULENCE ALERT

I attended a pitch meeting for an angel investor group. One of the founders came forward to pitch his business and shared a well-told story that showcased his interesting business.

Then he opened it up for questions, and by the end of his first answer, his tone had completely changed. With each question and answer, he sounded more frustrated, angry, and defensive. He obviously felt like he was answering the questions clearly, but his meaning was still unclear to the rest of us, so the audience asked the same questions in different ways, to the founder's palpable irritation.

When someone presents to a room full of angel investors who are listening to ten different pitches and can invest in one or none of those businesses, they create a challenge for themself if the audience can tell they're defensive or short-tempered. Through his tone, this founder clearly communicated frustration, and this was his parting message—not his amazing business idea, his great leadership, or his vision. His tone completely undermined his pitch.

Your mindset shows up in the tone of an email as well. We rush through emails or try to quickly "knock them out," but the resulting tone may be short, dismissive, and distracted.

Changing your tone in writing—or in any setting, frankly—starts with your intention, because what's going on in your head will come out on the screen or on the page. If you're running late to a meeting but you need to respond to an email before you go, your intention is "I need to get this email out of the way," and that will come out as terse and abrupt. Before you start typing, slow down and think about how you want to come across. Set an intention in your mind to direct your fingers. This is especially important if the person you are emailing doesn't know you well. If they know you, they can almost hear your tone in the email. But if they don't, major turbulence can result.

My father had a sarcastic wit, which I have inherited. Those who know me can hear my sarcastic tone if I use it in an email. I can't, however, use sarcasm with individuals who don't know me; they might mistake my messaging as curt or even rude. To ensure I have the right tone in an email, I write my message and then go back to the top and add an opening sentence to set the tone. Taking time to monitor your tone in emails may not seem particularly important; however, not doing so can create conflict, disengagement, and even lost business.

If you are growing a business, a division, or a team, you will have days where you feel angry, frustrated, defensive, or stressed. That's the nature of being an entrepreneurial leader. Being aware of how you show up when you feel those things is powerful as it enables you to ensure those tough days are not reflected in your tone, undermining your credibility in the process. Your tone can burn a bridge, alienate a crowd, or charm a snake. This makes tone a very powerful tool in your toolkit.

Visual (Body Language)

Many insightful books discuss the science of body language, and I've listed some in the Dig Deeper section at the end of this chapter. Here, I want to focus on body language in terms of its relevance to credibility and how it can play a part in creating turbulence for you and your team.

TURBULENCE ALERT

Ted had run a successful public advocacy business for twenty years. He had worked with major players in and out of state, but he was always shut out of the really big deals. Despite having a great track record, he could never quite make it into the top room, and he didn't understand what was holding him back.

I met him at a coffee shop for our initial discovery conversation. I asked him about his situation, what he saw as his biggest challenges, and what he ultimately wanted to achieve in our work together.

Ted hunched down over the table, clasped his fists together, and almost in a whisper said, "I want to command a room."

Sitting across from me in that coffee shop, Ted could not have made himself smaller. He embodied the exact opposite of commanding a room. It was almost like he was terrified of saying the words "I want to command a room" aloud.

Ted's body language undermined his goal. With me, he whispered and appeared hunched over, so I could only imagine how he showed up with people who were at the top of their game nationally. I didn't have to be in a room with him and a client to know why they loved his work but couldn't see him as the guy deserving a seat in the top room.

A great deal of body language has to do with our animal brain: our physical presence reflects what's going on in our minds. When we are afraid, we make ourselves small. When we are defensive, we cross our arms in front of our body as a way of putting up our defenses. When we are excited, we move quickly and likely make more eye contact when talking with others because we want them to be excited, too. We may not actually say, "I am feeling defensive" or "I'm excited about this prospect," but our body language communicates what's going on inside.

Turbulence around body language can show up when what we say doesn't match our body's visual cues. I had a tall client, who was a nice guy but also tended to be visually passive aggressive. When he met with someone in his office, he would have the person sit down while he remained standing and loomed over them, literally using his body language to encourage the person to accept his point of view. Employees found it hard to engage or trust him. His words indicated a willingness to be helpful and his tone sounded supportive, but his body language communicated mistrust and need for control. His presence undermined his message.

Energy

The fourth aspect of presence, which I've added to Mehrabian's original three, is energy. Although no one can quantify this aspect, people instinctively understand what it is and the fact that it plays a crucial part in executive credibility.

We use many phrases to describe energy, such as, "I'm getting a bad vibe from him" or "He sucked all the air out of the room." A positive comment about energy might be, "She's really driven," or centered, enthusiastic, focused, gregarious, and so on. One of my favorite words around energy is patience, which may not seem like an energy word at first glance. However, being patient requires you to slow down, focus, and take the time to direct your energy. People with patient energy generally convey a relaxed confidence that strengthens their credibility.

Energy is a big part of how we are perceived, and we all have a default setting. One person's default might be engaging and dynamic, while another person's might be slower—more deliberate and thoughtful. There is no good or bad. We simply need to be aware of our own default setting, as well as the triggers that can rev up our energy or slow it down. In addition, depending on the audience or the message we're trying to convey, we may want to consciously dial up or rein in our energy as it best serves us.

Our energy also changes day to day. Different forces and events can inform the vibe we bring into a room, meeting, or call. Stress, good news, or even a bad night's sleep can play a part in how we show up. In rapidly growing companies, energy seems to rev at a high pace all the time. Decision making needs to happen quickly. The constant evaluation and iteration can add stress, even exhaustion. However, when we engage with others, it is important that we be aware that our energy aligns with our message and our mission.

TURBULENCE ALERT

I worked with a bright and energetic client who was on the verge of making partner at a prestigious law firm. Kimberly had moved up the ladder quickly, which added to her perceived energy, and she was always engaging and dynamic.

Before Kimberly made partner, people seemed to appreciate the momentum and energy she brought to the firm. Now, as she sat in a room full of partners, Kimberly became aware that her energy did not fit. Even though she had achieved her goal, the reality was that her energy did not align with the slow, plodding energy of the partners who were satisfied with their success and not interested in innovation. Although not a founder, she was an entrepreneurial leader. She needed an outlet for not just her innovative ideas but also her energy.

Within the year, Kimberly found a position as general counsel for a late-stage startup. The leadership team's energy matched her own, and she knew she had made the right decision.

STREAMLINING STRATEGIES

I'm sure many of you read this section and thought, "Well, that's great. How do I manage my tone, body language, or energy? I have enough on my plate." Agreed. The goal of this book is to be helpful, not make work harder. So here are a few ways to start assessing and addressing how you show up.

Watch for Tone: Yours and Theirs

Phone calls provide an excellent opportunity to watch for tone.

If vocal qualities account for 38 percent of how we are perceived in person, you can imagine how much that percentage goes up when we are on the phone. The listener has no visual cues, so our credibility, and even authenticity, are determined by our tone as much as by what we say. If you don't believe me, put on a foreign film, close your eyes, and try to determine the nature of the conversation strictly based on tone. Since you can't understand what they say, their tone becomes the sole means of communication.

Now turn the exercise around and listen to the tone others use with you. Doing so can give you valuable information. If your client is pleased, their tone will be open and not rushed. Everyone is chattier when they are in a good mood. This is great time to get to know them better and find some common ground. If your boss's tone is abrupt and distracted, keep your message concise and to the point. They are likely in no mood for bad news, new ideas, or long conversations.

Tomorrow on your phone calls, make notes about the tone of each person on the call. I use UberConference, which records all of my client calls. When listening to the recordings, I find it very helpful to note anything in my client's tone I might have missed on the call. I also listen to my own tone and where it might have been helpful or where I may have undermined myself. And yes, as much as I work on this, tone mishaps happen to me, too.

Leverage a Keyword Assessment

I have scoured the industry for an assessment that I could use in helping clients understand their current executive presence. I've found two to be most helpful: one is the DISC assessment discussed in Chapter 1) and the other is a simple one-page keyword assessment I created. Both assessments use descriptors or keywords to cover many of the qualities that inform leaders' executive presence. As I mentioned in Chapter 1, the DISC assessment can provide insights into how we may be perceived. My own keyword assessment hones in more specifically on words and descriptors that reflect how we embody tone, body language, and energy in our presence, for example, abrupt, dynamic, judgmental, and reliable.

After you create your own keyword assessment, you can leverage it to inform your executive presence:

- *Step 1*: Share your keyword assessment with two or three people with whom you work. I suggest choosing individuals who know you in different contexts (peers, bosses, employees, board members, clients) and then fill it out for yourself as well. Each person should choose three words that describe you at that moment and three words they would like to see you embody during the next year. Keeping it to three words ensures the words are prioritized.
- *Step 2*: Assess the words. How closely do your words align with those chosen by others? How do the words chosen by managers compare with those chosen by board members or clients? Are you showing up in the same way with peers and with those senior or junior to you? Do you present yourself in the same way to those inside as well as outside the organization?
- *Step 3*: Plan next steps. If there is misalignment in chosen words, then the goal is to figure out which elements of your presence are showing up in a way that undermines you and make a shift so your presence supports you and your position. For example, do you need to adjust your energy, or

would a shift in your body language make a difference? If there is alignment, then the goal is to consider any necessary shifts from how you are currently perceived to how you need to be perceived to move your organization or your career to the next level.

Let's say others see the leader as *thorough*, a word that reflects systematic thinking and attention to detail and possibly working at a slower pace. Thoroughness is an excellent trait, and no one should stop being thorough. However, if people can choose just three words to describe the CEO of a rapidly growing organization, should *thorough* be one of them? Possibly, but even still, *thorough* might not be *the* quality with which a CEO wants to lead or it may not be right for this organization. With this information in hand, the leader could choose another descriptor from the "future" list, one that does not invalidate their thorough quality but supports a more dynamic part of their presence. A word like *decisive* might be more effective. Being seen as decisive does not mean not being seen as thorough. It simply means that one descriptor is prioritized over another.

Any descriptor or keyword embodies a tone, a pace, a way of moving, and an energy. Thoroughness, for example, might be seen as quiet, methodical, and "head down," looking at the details. A leader described as distracted might show up as high energy, moving from idea to idea, and their body language might be seen as open and expressive. It is helpful to break down each word, understand how it is perceived and whether that serves you, and then see where you need to put your intention to make a shift. It's also important to know that there are no good or bad keywords. Each one has a dark and a light side. Each may reflect a much-needed quality or a trait that may be creating turbulence.

TURBULENCE ALERT

Christina is a bright executive who took over an organization that had been in crisis. The previous head had been in the role for quite some time, and he had been failing in every metric. During his tenure, he had lost support from the team due to his poor leadership, but he had, over the years, strengthened relationships with various influential board members.

After he was fired and Christina joined the organization, she had to establish her credibility with her team, her board, and her customers. She also had the additional challenge of working with an "old boy" network board in an "old boy" network industry. As a result, despite her successes with increasing revenue and engagement, from the board she sensed a lack of trust, questions about her credibility, and worst of all, sexism. She decided to work toward elevating her presence to support not just her organizational but also her professional growth.

Christina's goal keywords were *influential*, *trusted*, and *qualified*. *Trusted* and *qualified* were her response to the concerns she believed she faced, particularly with her board of directors. The truth is, the data showed she was very qualified, so we took that off the list and looked at the assessment responses she received from others in her organization. They described her as *smart*, *direct*, *reliable*, and *organized*—all good words, but the last two are more descriptive of a "doer" rather than a leader. These are certainly valuable skills that serve any leader, but this assessment focuses on the *top three* keywords, and a leader in Christina's position wouldn't want *reliable* and *organized* to be two of them. Christina needed to elevate her presence to match her elevated role. To this end, we looked at the "words for future growth" section, which included *persuasive*, *open*, and *confident*. These gave us a place to focus our presence work.

Another word other people selected for future growth was *warm*. In discussing this word with Christina, we realized that any perceived lack of warmth was likely due to her sense that she had to prove herself as a new leader, her battle with the stereotypes of women in leadership, and her personal style, which is direct and efficient. It wasn't that she lacked warmth; it was simply that her energy, organization, and drive were perceived as such. This perception could cause turbulence and prevent her from being perceived as *influential* and *trusted*. Rather than work on being *warm*, we landed on the word *engaging*, since that is more authentic for Christina and, crucially, more effective for her role.

We started to work on her executive presence, moving from *direct*, *organized*, and *reliable* to *influential*, *trusted*, and *engaging*. Christina chose one word at a time on which to work. For *engaging*, we defined some metrics with which she could track her progress on moving the needle on that keyword, and then we defined how she could embody the word:

- Body language: Christina worked on increasing her eye contact to be seen as present, both physically and mentally. She also tried to interact personally (versus email) whenever possible and minimize her multitasking when meeting with others.
- Tone: Direct leaders can get things done, but they also risk being perceived as curt or dismissive. Christina focused on sharing her thought processes rather than simply stating decisions. She also became more aware of how her tone showed up in meetings and calls.
- Energy: Christina's direct and efficient style reflected a fast energy. She focused on slowing down in staff meetings, board meetings, and even when creating her to-do list.

Focusing on one word at a time allowed Christina to begin to shift her executive presence. Once her success metrics and executive presence were aligned, her credibility and influence strengthened. In addition, as Christina moved from doer to leader, the "old boys" on the board began to view her as a peer. Coupled with her already excellent work, this shift gained her the buy-in and collaborative environment she needed.

Let's look at the word *quick-minded*, which can lend itself both to strengths and to potential turbulence. A quick-minded person might be seen as highly verbal, strong at engaging off the cuff, comfortable making eye contact, and animated. These qualities are helpful for brainstorming meetings. The individual is likely able to quickly condense thoughts or ideas. They may be seen as decisive and good in a crisis.

On the other hand, in some situations a quick-minded person may be perceived as too verbal and as an interrupter. Decisions may be made so quickly that others may not feel their option has been taken into account.

In one situation or one organization, quick-mindedness may be a valued quality; in another, it may not. Next steps depend on the person's specific scenario. For example, if someone isn't perceived as quick-minded in an organization where that quality would be helpful, they might:

- Begin engaging in off-the-cuff contributions.
- Use decisive language.
- Increase eye contact.

However, if their quick-mindedness is creating turbulence, the individual might:

- Ensure they are fully present with others (engage in active listening).
- Be aware of interrupting.
- Ensure others feel valued/heard.
- Slow down and ask questions like, "Any questions so far?" to ensure others are following.

Making small shifts in our nonverbal communication is never about being something we are not. It is simply about highlighting the qualities that serve us in our role and elevate our presence and credibility.

Craft an Intention

When actors bring a character to life, they often go through the script and highlight words and descriptions other characters and the playwright use to describe their character—much like the keyword assessment just described. They make choices about how the character moves, their energy level, and their tone of voice with different characters or in different scenes. Then they layer in nonverbal elements that reflect the actor's personal beliefs and abilities as well as the director's take.

This prep work must take place before opening night because once they are on stage with an audience, actors can no longer actively think about their body language or tone of voice. At that point, they use a few tools to help them remain in character whatever happens, and the most powerful of these tools is intention. Once an actor has defined the tone, energy, and body language of their character, they craft one intention that will allow them to embody the desired presence. There may be one intention per scene and one overarching intention for their character in the play; either way, it is what drives and informs everything else.

Leaders can do the same. Once you have identified how your tone, energy, and body language may need to shift, you can craft an intention to support your role, your situation, or your goals.

Your intention is essentially what you are communicating to yourself, which we touched on in Chapter 1. It is like the mantra that informs your body language, tone, and energy. To craft the right intention, you need to answer three questions:

1. What do I want to achieve?
2. What are the likely objections or challenges I will face?
3. What kind of presence do I need to convey to ensure I achieve my goal?

Without taking the time to deliberately craft this intention, you run the risk of communicating an "unintended" intention that undermines your goal. We always have an intention in our mind—whether subconscious or meticulously crafted, it's there. If you walk into a meeting thinking, "I want to get out of here as quickly as possible," that's going to inform your body language. It's likely that your body will at least partially face the door. You likely won't chime in unless absolutely necessary, and when you do, you will probably provide short answers because you don't want to get into a long, drawn-out conversation. You may not have consciously set the intention of getting out of the room as quickly as possible, but that's what you will communicate because that's what your body language and tone will reflect.

Our body language, tone, and energy are informed by our animal brain—instinct. All three are a reflection of what's going on in our mind. To make sure these facets of presence don't undermine our credibility, we have to slow down and craft an intention using the three clarifying questions. That's how we level up and avoid conflict.

Let's say you want to get buy-in on a big opportunity, but you haven't taken the time to craft the right intention. If you walk in thinking, "I'm going to hammer home my reasons," you might end up using a tone that sounds harsh or too aggressive. Or if you think, "This is a shoo-in," you might end up rushing through the pitch. You might also fail to actively listen to what is asked or what is not.

However, if you walk in with the intention, "I want to get them excited about the plan I'm laying out," there is a higher likelihood of engaging fully, walking them through your thought process, and actively listening for unspoken messages of agreement or enthusiasm. You can probably hold your intention for twenty to thirty minutes with ease, but if you have a really long meeting, I suggest writing your intention on a sticky note or on your pad so you can periodically glance at it, touch base with your goal, and then reengage in the conversation.

Next time you go to a networking event, try this experiment. Look for people who are facing each other and talking. Then look at their feet. When people are truly engaged in that conversation, both feet will be facing the person with whom they are speaking, and they will be making direct eye contact. If, however, someone has one foot facing in a different direction (they have one foot out the door) or if they are quickly scanning the room, you can bet they're looking for a way to end the conversation, either by inviting others to join or by trying to step away.

If you think your body language or tone or energy are undermining you or not serving you, craft an intention that allows your goal keywords to show up.

BEING PRESENT

Being present is a term you have likely heard, and it goes hand in hand with active listening. However, although there is a physical component of being present, it is the mental component that elevates, informs, and supports how we lead. I like to think of it as being "bright eyed and bushy tailed."

PHYSICAL

In my experience, the most successful restaurants are run by owners who make their presence felt in the restaurant, and that starts by being physically present with regularity. By doing this often, owners can make their presence felt even when they are not physically there. The staff has a clearer sense of what is expected, and they know what the owner wants guests to experience. Conversely, if owners are never physically present, employees get into their own routines, and guests experience inconsistent service or meals. It's hard to ensure efficient service, consistent food, and contented guests when no leadership is present.

Finding ways to make your presence felt is essential for your teams. In Chapter 6 on teams, I'll cover some ways you can do this in the office and virtually.

However, being physically present does not guarantee being perceived as truly present, attentive, or engaged. We have all sat through the staff meeting where half the team, and sometimes even the leader, are not all there. Being present physically but not mentally does more damage to your credibility than if you hadn't shown up in the first place.

MENTAL

With an increasingly virtual workforce, remaining present with our teams requires creativity. Meeting apps like Zoom allow us to have a virtual presence, but making our presence felt (whether we are physically there or not) entails taking the time and energy to ensure we are mentally present.

This is exhausting; I get it. Listening actively involves always being on. After just a week of working from home in 2020, everyone understood that a day of Zoom calls is much more tiring than a day of live meetings. Why? Virtual video calls require more energy to remain fully present. You feel all eyes are on you, so looking away quickly or slipping out the back of the room isn't possible.

I never do full-day workshops, partly because I don't believe anyone can digest six to eight hours of new information in one sitting, but mostly because both the audience and I need to remain fully present, and that's incredibly hard to do for eight hours. We can't be mentally "on" for a full day.

Why have a meeting if you're not going to be present? Showing up and being fully engaged for five minutes of the meeting is more valuable than sitting through the whole hour while you review documents or think about the next items on your list.

If you're not fully present, chances are you're going to get caught—someone asks you a question that you don't hear, or you go over territory that's already been discussed, or you simply look out of touch with the conversation at hand, all of which can seriously undermine your credibility.

Being fully present also gives you a chance to listen for ways people are communicating: who isn't speaking up, who is looking away when the question is asked, who is taking up all the oxygen, who looks uncomfortable. Being fully present means you're reading all the signals others may send—body language, tone, the vibe in the room, even who may be staying silent though they clearly have something to say. Only when we are fully present can our senses be alert enough to take in all of this data.

Being mentally present isn't about being on 24/7. It's about being intentional in how, when, and why we show up and being fully engaged when we do.

TURBULENCE ALERT

I worked with a CEO who used to fly into town for big quarterly meetings and then proceeded to scroll through his phone or step out for ten minutes at a time. Bill was physically there but not mentally. His COO would lead these meetings with a clear agenda and actively engage team members to contribute. Bill would randomly chime in, often covering ground that had already been discussed or taking the conversation off on a tangent. His team hated these meetings. They went on forever and often ended without a clear plan of action.

Bill told me that these meetings were too long and that many of the agenda items were handled by others on his leadership team. He felt it was important to be physically present but believed that much of the content was not relevant to him.

After we began working together, I suggested that Bill choose the agenda items on which he wanted to contribute and get feedback. The agenda was then drafted so those items were scheduled together. I then suggested that he choose to attend at either the beginning or the end of the meeting. This would ensure he could either kick off the day or wrap things up. More importantly, it allowed him to attend to the issues he believed to be critical and leave when they were done.

The effect of this plan for Bill was that he felt the meeting was more focused and productive. The effect for the team was the same, and they found his presence more compelling and inspirational. A win-win for everyone.

STREAMLINING STRATEGIES

We can create so much turbulence for ourselves and our organizations when we are not present. You may miss crucial data or points of view. Members of your team may feel unheard. Those same team members may see you as being present with others and unresponsive to them alone. Your board may sense your exhaustion or distraction and perceive it as lack of confidence or dismissiveness. Your tone and energy may put off some from engaging fully or honestly. None of these serve you or your organization.

I'm not going to tell you that being fully present is easy. Being present is a muscle that can be built up, and you can get better every day, but it will take effort, intention, and stamina. Here are some practical strategies to work on being fully present, physically and mentally.

Make Eye Contact

The most powerful tool in your toolkit is eye contact, whether you are in a meeting or talking with someone in the hallway. It is hard to daydream when you are making direct eye contact with someone—not impossible, but it is very, very hard. I even do this on Zoom calls. I look straight into the camera so that for my client, it feels like I am making direct eye contact. It also helps me focus on what they are saying and how they are engaging with me.

Put a Pin in It

If you have a million things on your plate, you're probably running five to ten minutes late to every meeting, and that's understandable. Once you are in the meeting or on a call, however, find a way to leave the previous meeting or call behind so you can fully focus on the present conversation.

Before you shift tasks, put a pin in that last thing so you can focus on the present one. That might mean jotting notes about the last meeting to get them out of your head. I like to voice-record my thoughts. The important thing is to not let the musings or problem solving from the past meeting or conversation creep into the present one.

Schedule a Ten-Minute Buffer

To give myself time to slow down and focus on the purpose of an upcoming meeting or conversation, I give myself a ten-minute buffer ahead of each one. During that time, I ask myself, "What do I want to achieve in this meeting? With whom am I speaking? How do I need to communicate with this person?" Then I craft an intention that supports my internal agenda and moves me into the next conversation with the appropriate focus.

Give yourself the time to ensure your message is clear and top of mind so you can effectively engage and get the most out of your valuable time.

Record and Review

It can be challenging to remain present when taking notes or viewing documents when you are on a call. I like to record important phone or Zoom calls so I can fully focus on my client, their tone, body language, and subtext. Then I go back and listen to the recording to make notes. Not only can I remain present with the other person, but when listening later, I often catch things I missed.

Reschedule if Necessary

If you have a big meeting in the afternoon or something will take all your headspace, you might need to acknowledge your inability to be fully present at the other meetings on your calendar. If you can't be fully present, reschedule when possible. Let the person or group know that you need to focus and prepare for the upcoming presentation or meeting. Tell them you value their time. Ask if they would be willing to reschedule.

If someone has made time in their calendar but you haven't made time in your brain, then having the meeting doesn't do either of you any good. It will actually undermine you because you will show up as someone who isn't connected or present, doesn't care, isn't listening, or doesn't think the other person is important. That doesn't serve you and only causes turbulence.

Contribute Meaningfully

I am a talkative person, so I am lucky to have found a career that requires me to be highly verbal. There are times, however, where my talkativeness gets in the way of listening and undermines me.

When I was on the board of a particular nonprofit, we received the agenda in advance. When the meetings came, I was prepared to speak up on the different agenda items and contribute where I thought it important. I came to realize that although I contributed out of a desire to be helpful and bring value, I put in my two cents a bit too often. As a result, I was heard on almost nothing. I undermined my value and, by extension, my credibility.

So I tried something different. I started looking at the agenda in advance and deciding the points on which I really wanted to be heard. Then I bit my lip (sometimes literally at first) or kept my hand over my mouth to stop myself from contributing too often. When we reached the item about which I felt strongly, I was seen as an active listener and ultimately had a greater impact.

I own the fact that I'm still improving in this area. I find that in working virtually, my habit of taking ten minutes before a meeting to form my intention has taken a hit, and as a result I sometimes have to mute myself and refocus on where I want to add value. Your challenge may be the opposite. I've had bright, dynamic clients who are happy to only listen. They are thoughtful and methodical and don't want to contribute until they have had the time to process. However, this can undermine them, too. I ask these leaders to take time ahead of a meeting to pick one agenda item on which they want to speak. Then during the meeting, they jump in at that moment, make their contribution, and jump back out. This allows not only their contribution to be heard but their presence to be felt.

Speaking up and being heard are two sides of the same coin. To bring value and be seen as present, you need to let others in. To do that, you need to find a way to contribute that works for you and supports your goals.

Try Improv

If you are unused to or uncomfortable with being fully present, I suggest taking improvisation classes. Improv requires you to be diligently present, speak up on the spot, and listen closely to the others on stage. A scene dies if one team member isn't present. The same can happen in a meeting or a call. Although this may seem an outside-the-box tool, it has worked every time with my clients.

SLOW DOWN TO SPEED UP

There is a reason the conversations, books, and trainings around executive presence are becoming more and more common. It is not that presence hasn't always been fundamental to a leader's credibility and ability to command influence. It is simply that in the past, a discussion of presence was often reduced to what you wear. However, assessing and leveraging the science (yes, it is a science) of nonverbal communication, once viewed as something for actors and academics, is now understood to be a powerful tool for leaders in business—if they take the time to leverage it.

Next, we'll discuss how to leverage storytelling to streamline growth and elevate your influence.

TURBULENCE TOOLKIT

Assess

- When I walk into a meeting with my team, do I command the room?
- Do different stakeholders' perceptions of me align?
- Does my current executive presence align with how I want/need to be perceived?
- Are my mindset and my executive presence aligned?
- Do I embody the keywords that define my current role?
- What feedback have I received that might provide insight into my nonverbal communication?
- Do I embody the keywords for the next level of leadership?
- Do I tune out in certain meetings?
- Does my team feel my presence even when I am not physically present?
- Do I rush from meeting to meeting or call to call?
- How does my executive presence shift when things go wrong or I'm stressed?

Be Intentional

- Be honest with yourself about how you show up and ask those you trust to do the same.
- Ensure you are in the best quadrant on the Confidence Matrix to support your leadership.
- Be aware of how you're showing up but never critical or judgmental.
- List out the qualities you embody, where and when they serve you, and when they may undermine you.
- Identify your keywords for the year and how to embody them visually, vocally, and with your energy.

Slow down to speed up so you can be intentional with others.

Identify strategies that allow you to replenish your energy so you can be fully present.

Pick One Thing

- Keyword assessment
- Body language
- Tone
- Energy
- Intention
- Being present

Dig Deeper

- *The Actor and the Text* by Cecily Berry
- *Credibility: How Leaders Gain and Lose It, Why People Demand It* by James M. Kouzes and Barry Z. Posner
- *The Definitive Book on Body Language: Win Every Day with Nonverbal Communication Secrets* by Allan and Barbara Pease
- *Executive Presence: The Art of Commanding Respect Like a CEO* by Harrison Monarth
- *Executive Presence: The Missing Link between Merit and Success* by Sylvia Ann Hewlett
- *The Journal of the Institute of Knowledge Management*
- *The Power of Presence: What Actors Can Teach Business Leaders* by Christopher Von Baeyer
- *Thrive: The Third Metric to Redefining Success and Creating a Life of Well-Being, Wisdom, and Wonder* by Arianna Huffington
- Join an acting or improv class

CHAPTER 4

STORYTELLING

NARRATIVES GIVE INFORMATION CONTEXT

"Tell me the facts and I'll learn. Tell me the truth and I'll believe. But tell me a story and it will live in my heart forever."

—NATIVE AMERICAN PROVERB

In moviemaking, the director is a storyteller. Though the screenwriter crafts the script, it's the director who crafts the narrative. Through storyboarding, casting, lighting, editing, and other conscious decisions, the director creates the mood, theme, and ultimate message received by the audience. To effectively communicate their intended message, the director has to know how they want to affect an audience and how to take the words on the page to create that effect. They arrange, rearrange, and even omit scenes so the narrative progresses in the desired sequence and pace. They use the camera angles, music, and lighting to direct the focus of the audience to the character, environment, or mood that brings the viewer to the intended conclusion.

It is no different for you as a leader. Every time you communicate, whether it's a staff meeting, a pitch, a speech at a conference, or a one-on-one conversation, you can leverage storytelling to engage others, craft the desired narrative, and set the tone for the actions or beliefs you want to inspire in others. Yes, words are important, and you should make sure the script is tight, well written, and focused on the right information. But how you organize the examples, testimonials, data, and statistics—the "scenes" of your movie, so to speak—as well as what you put in and leave out all becomes part of the narrative itself.

Storytelling is a commonly used buzzword in business today, but many leaders don't understand how or when to use this tool to their advantage. They also don't realize that by becoming a great storyteller, they can avoid or manage all types of turbulence.

Stories give information context. They provide the thread that connects ideas, data, and outcomes. They allow you to highlight your message or conversation with the narrative you want to communicate. Dr. Howard Gardner, professor at Harvard University, has said, "Stories constitute the single most powerful weapon in a leader's arsenal."[12]

Storytelling is the element of my actor's toolkit I draw from the most. It's the secret sauce I provide clients. In this chapter, we'll unpack how you can leverage this tool in every conversation, email, and pitch. In addition, I'll lay out a formula to help you consistently craft persuasive stories and effectively lead your audience to The One Thing you want them to know, think, do, or believe.

---

12   Jeff Boudens, Rodgers Palmer, and Brooke Weddle, "Mobilize Your Organization with a Powerful Change Story," McKinsey Organization Blog, October 28, 2019, https://www. mckinsey.com/business-functions/organization/our-insights/the-organization-blog/ mobilize-your-organization-with-a-powerful-change-story#.

REDEFINING STORYTELLING

When a company or career grows and changes rapidly, it is easy to simply state facts, share metrics, or highlight data. However, as the leader of a company, a department, or your own career, you can use stories to more easily and quickly share information, get buy-in, and unify company culture. A story is like a suitcase into which the listener can easily pack away the data points, effortlessly carry it, and readily open it to share with others.

Storytelling is in our DNA as people. It was part of human civilization long before books were written. From Greek mythology to Shakespeare's plays to the golden age of moviemaking to Instagram stories, storytelling taps into how our brains naturally work. MRI studies in neuroscience and the effects of storytelling on the brain show how many different areas of the brain light up when someone is listening to a narrative. In other words, stories engage the full brain.[13] They're how we prefer to hear and share information.

Some people have the misconception that storytelling is merely about listing information or events. I attended a large conference where the keynote speaker had clearly been told to start her speech with a story. She narrated a series of events that happened on a particular day, but I have no idea what message her "story" was supposed convey to the audience or what lesson we were supposed to take away. A series of events or list of facts is not a story. Effective storytelling requires giving those facts context and meaning to the listener. As in ancient storytelling,

---

13 Raymond A. Mar, "The Neural Basis of Social Cognition and Storytelling," Annual Review of Psychology 62 (2011): 22.

it is the moral of your story, not the events, that make it work. There is even science to prove it.[14]

LEVERAGING STORYTELLING TO STREAMLINE GROWTH

In her book *Stories That Stick*, Kindra Hall says that stories help leaders bridge the gap between the target audience and a business's products, services, or even the leaders themselves. The vision of your business is a story. The company culture is a story. A sales pitch or investor pitch is a story. Stories can persuade, inspire, and soothe.

If you approach any of these situations without taking the time to craft a compelling story, you risk loss of sales, lack of motivation on your team, and failure to get buy-in for critical situations.

Here are some ways you can leverage storytelling to support your growth.

VISION STORY

We've spent some time on company vision and why clarity is essential to ensure the organization has a clear path to growth. Once the vision is clear to you and you have ensured you can make it clear to others, take it one step further and craft a *vision story*.

If the vision statement is the destination, then the vision story

---

14   Ye Yuan, Judy Major-Girardin, and Steven Brown, "Storytelling Is Intrinsically Mentalistic: A Functional Magnetic Resonance Imaging Study of Narrative Production across Modalities," Journal of Cognitive Neuroscience 30, no. 9 (2018): 1298–1314, https://doi.org/10.1162/jocn_a_01294.

is the journey to that destination. Whether it takes the form of a strategic plan or a rousing speech given at the annual meeting, the vision story allows people to commit and follow you.

A good place to begin is with your origin story. Much like the films about beloved Marvel characters, these origin stories help the audience or listener understand or simply remember the *why*: Why we do what we do. Why we make the choices we make. Why this is the direction we are going to take. If your vision statement is honest and accurate, it should be founded on the why. Then your story can move on to the how—the events, offerings, or culture that ensure you move closer to attaining your vision.

As your organization grows and iterates, you will find your story does as well. You will have new anecdotes, new markets, or expanded perspective. It will likely not be a new story, just one with new chapters.

The most compelling vision stories allow others to see themselves on the journey with you. The vision story allows you to add color, landmarks, and important characters. The fastest way to engage anyone in what you're doing, from a team member to a board member to an investor, is through your vision story.

As you will see later in this chapter, I believe it is important to address the elephant in the room when one exists, so let me do that here. You might be thinking it would be helpful to have an example of a vision story, in contrast with a vision statement. Vision stories have multiple layers and levels and are crafted for various stakeholders. They also tend to be quite long. The fastest way to share an example is point you to YouTube, where Anita

Roddick, founder of The Body Shop, shares her vision story in a thirty-minute video.[15]

Roddick's story is an excellent illustration because it shows both her personal vision (to "make a living for herself and her two daughters while her husband was away travelling"[16]) and her company vision ("Business can be a source for good"[17]). It's not a surprise that the company "lost its way" after it was purchased by L'Oréal and Roddick's original vision, personal and organizational, was no longer part of its journey.[18]

VALUE STORY

You can leverage multiple value stories across the organization to motivate, inspire, engage, and elevate. In the chapter on clarity, we discussed the importance of knowing and articulating the value *you* bring to your organization. It's important to craft a clear narrative about your own value and to iterate it as necessary based on changes in the company and the role in which you find yourself.

As with the movie director, the story of your value is not only based on the script determined by your words. Although the right word is powerful, a written bio is not necessarily a narrative of your value. Most bios read like a list of roles, companies, or awards, not a story that takes the reader on a journey. They speak to a person's credentials, not necessarily their value.

---

15 PSONA Films, "Anna Roddick—My Story (The Body Shop)," YouTube, posted March 15, 2016, https://www.youtube.com/watch?v=Dpq4SyNbUbY.

16 Katie Hope, "The Body Shop: What Went Wrong?" BBC News, February 9, 2017, https://www.bbc.com/news/business-38905530.

17 The Body Shop, "Our Story," n.d., https://www.thebodyshop.com/en-gb/about-us/our-story/a/a00002.

18 Hope, "The Body Shop."

TURBULENCE ALERT

Years ago, I had a big tech company as a client. Twice a month I held office hours where anyone at the company could sign up to for coaching. Inevitably, half of my slots were filled by younger team members who wanted me to coach them in asking for a raise.

I quickly realized none had taken the time to craft a value story. In these sessions, my first question was always the same: "Why are you more valuable today than when you were first hired or when you received your last raise?" Many times, the person didn't have an answer or would say something like "I've been here for nine months." That story doesn't show value. We would work together to co-create a narrative that highlighted the ways they had added top- or bottom-line value to the organization. We found data points to support their narrative of value to the team—ways they showed initiative and leadership or solved a critical problem. That became a value story they could share. It also helped them keep an eye out for other chapters they could add to their value story in the future.

I recommend crafting several value stories in advance so you are ready to share them in media interviews, staff meetings, and mentoring relationships. Each value story can bring unique color and context to your experience and job history through shared understanding and evocative word choices.

There are, however, other value stories—narratives you can craft that allow your team to understand the value of their current endeavor. When rolling out new plans or initiatives, getting the team on board and rowing together isn't always smooth. A value story can show your team or your board that plan's value to the organization and to them. It so often happens that plans or decisions are announced and then, that's it. Sure, you'll hear timelines and budgets, but often there's no discussion of value. The why behind a decision or initiative can engage and motivate the team.

You may already think of sales conversations as value stories—your top salespeople do—but what about interviews? When you are assessing a candidate, you can share a value story about the organization, the role, or the culture. You may think the candidate is ideal, but if your value story doesn't speak to them or if they don't believe they are aligned, it's better for both of you to know that before they are hired rather than six months later.

As startups grow, institutional investors will often (and too often unwisely) consider bringing in a new CEO who brings a "different skillset," one they believe is required to continue to scale. In that moment, founders must have a clear narrative regarding their value to the organization so they can articulate it to the board. Investors have no problem replacing founders if they see greater value in bringing in someone else. This is turbulence everyone would rather avoid.

Take the time to ask yourself, "What do I bring to the team? How can my value be measured? What is the moral of my story? What value does my leadership bring to my company?" If you don't know or can't articulate these things, you are potentially undermining your credibility and leadership. (Look back at Chapter 2 for a refresher on clarifying your value.) The culmination of your answers becomes the building blocks of your value story.

THE PITCH STORY

Pitching—whether it's an investor pitch, sales pitch, or elevator pitch—is nothing but a story, told not to secure a new client or funding but simply to secure more time. Think of a pitch as the trailer to your movie. It piques the interest and gets the audience excited to hear more. However, even the trailer has to tell a story, and everyone in the organization should be telling the same version. Leaders need to make sure that every employee who gives an elevator pitch, sales pitch, or investor pitch shares the same concise, focused, and compelling narrative about the company.

I have mentored hundreds of startups and helped them craft and deliver investor pitches, and the challenges are usually the same. One is that founders often tell the wrong story to their potential investors—"wrong" in that they tell the story of their product, not the story of their business. Because they spend every day deep in the product development and client conversations, founders tend to focus on products or services. They talk about features and benefits, and they show demos, all of which can give investors context, but the investor is considering buying the business, not the product. The product is certainly one chapter, but investors primarily want to know about the market, the competition and why this product is superior, how the founders are going to find new clients, and how they're going to make money.

In addition, founders often share too much. They mention everything they have done to date to highlight past successes, but a pitch should tell the story of who they will become, not who they have been. If the goal of the pitch is simply to secure more time, then founders need to show only the trailer, but they often want to show the whole movie.

Giving more information does not guarantee greater engagement or greater likelihood of enthusiasm. Any pitch should be brief and to the point. It should grab the listener's attention, get them to lean in, and hook them to meet again.

At the same time, the pitch story must also be consistent across the organization, from employee to employee. In my experience, leaders often open the door to some turbulence because narratives are not aligned and consistent across the organization. Take elevator pitches, for example. I have performed numerous company audits where I ask a cross section of employees to record their elevator pitch. I then edit the videos together so the leader can view them back-to-back. They are always shocked by the range of stories—it's like watching ten different films that have little to do with one other. One could easily believe the employees are speaking about different organizations.

As the leader, you want to give your employees the tools to tell the same unified story. The pitch must be crafted so that it leads people to the outcome, belief, or action that you want. Anyone who works with you and gives an investor, sales, or elevator pitch should be leading people to the same outcome, belief, or action. The moral of the story should be the same.

Is there a formula for crafting persuasive stories? I think so.

THE ONE THING FORMULA

Whether you're crafting a sales pitch, or telling the story of your value, or writing a speech for a conference, the following formula can help you craft stories that bring your audience to The One Thing you want them to know, think, do, or believe.

CONNECTION, CLARITY, CREDIBILITY

In the mid-350s BC, Aristotle published his *Art of Rhetoric*. In it he lays out his theory on persuasion, which at the end of the day is the goal of a story. He refers to the three elements of *pathos*, relating to persuasion through empathy; *logos*, or relating to persuasion through logic; and *ethos*, relating to persuasion through credibility and character. I call these elements *connection*, *clarity*, and *credibility*, and they are woven into The One Thing Formula presented in this section:

- Connection is all about your *audience*, discussed in step 1.
- Clarity is all about your *content*, discussed in steps 2 and 3.
- Credibility is all about *you*, discussed in step 4.

1. CONSIDER THE DNA OF YOUR AUDIENCE

In telling any story, you must consider your audience first, whether it is an audience of one or a thousand. We don't tell stories to hear ourselves talk (although I have listened to a few folks who do). We tell them to engage, inspire, inform, or motivate others. To achieve this, we need to know and understand the people before us, the audience.

Think about it this way: what happened on your trip to Vegas is what happened on your trip to Vegas, but the version you tell your mom will be different than the version you tell your best friend. Some of the content in both versions will likely be the same, but you will edit your narrative based on the audience.

To craft the right story for your audience, consider three facets of their DNA: demographics, needs, and attitude.

Demographics

Always think about demographics first: who are the people with whom you are communicating? Are they your investors? Are they employees? Is it your mother? Does their generation matter? How well do they know your business? How well do they know you?

A physician's conversation on a new medical breakthrough with colleagues differs from the same conversation with potential investors. Clarity on who is hearing your message is essential.

Needs

Next, consider the needs of your audience. Understanding in advance what questions, objections, or concerns your audience may bring with them will help you organize your message, front-load answers to any concerns, and ensure you address the questions and don't leave people uncertain, unclear, or frankly, bored.

Even in a one-on-one conversation, you are more likely to achieve your goals if you understand what your audience needs to know or the objections they might have. Ultimately, the story is not about what you want to say but about what they need to hear.

TURBULENCE ALERT

I worked with a large telecommunications company that was looking for a buyer. They crafted a broad story that highlighted their many successes. This story might have worked well if they were looking to sell to a competitor, because they had a great narrative regarding customer success metrics, strong IT and infrastructure, and a deeply experienced team.

However, the audience demographic was composed of teams from private equity firms. The needs of that group revolved almost exclusively around finances—margins, profits, and growth. This narrative was harder to sell because the company, though having grown year over year, was in the final phases of integrating an acquired competitor. The numbers were strong but didn't tell the full and compelling story these buyers wanted to hear. They wanted to learn about strong margins and soaring ARR (annual recurring revenue).

Ultimately, each department—sales, marketing, tech, and product—found a way to articulate how their successes, from client satisfaction to IT systems, could reinforce a compelling numbers-focused narrative. By considering the needs of their particular audience, they were able to secure a buyer.

Attitude

How we communicate with people largely depends on their attitude or mindset—where they are mentally and emotionally.

In 2020, virtual meetings became a part of our daily work life. A single introvert living alone and having to work from home will have a different attitude than someone newly working from home who's also watching three kids under the age of six. The way those two individuals digest information will be different, which requires crafting and delivering a different version of your story.

If you speak at conferences, you know there are two times when you would rather not speak: right after lunch, when everyone is groggy after eating chicken and pasta in cream sauce, and at the end of the day, when people are thinking about cocktail hour or catching their plane home. Audiences in both cases need to be engaged quickly. To make the needed connection, messaging should be brief and every effort made to bring listeners into the narrative early on. People want to see themselves in the story.

In another situation, you may walk into a presentation knowing that one or more attendees around the table have objections or misgivings. Understanding that helps you take those objections or concerns into account as you prepare your narrative. If you can quickly address and move those objections to one side, the likelihood of buy-in goes up.

TURBULENCE ALERT

I gave the keynote speech at a tech conference in London in June 2016, the day after the Brexit vote. Most people in London voted to Remain, so they were shocked by the vote to Leave. As a result, the conference was populated by walking zombies trying to process what had just happened.

I had to give a speech to this audience about innovation and persuasion. When preparing my talk, I had taken time to ask the organizer about attendees, I reached out to some colleagues who had attended in the past, and I worked to understand my audience and their needs. However, all that went out the window with the Brexit vote. I knew these attendees, mostly entrepreneurs and founders, were not in the frame of mind to learn strategies to persuade investors. The rug had just been pulled out from under them, and they didn't know whether they would even have a business going forward.

First, I had to figure out how to address the elephant in the room. To me, the elephant in the room is the big, obvious objection, obstacle, or question mark that stays in every listener's mind until it is addressed head-on. In this case, there was no way to start my speech without addressing the vote. It took up all the space in the room, both in terms of mood and energy, and I had to address it first, without allowing it to be the center of my speech.

Understanding that allowed me to take the story I had prepared and put it in the new context of the changes this elephant had created. My speech, which had centered on how entrepreneurs can use the ground rules of storytelling to persuade investors, had to shift. I opened my presentation by stating that I would rather spend the morning after the vote with entrepreneurs than any other group because they are risk tolerant, open to change, always looking for solutions, and doggedly persistent. Then I kept my content but shifted my focus to how entrepreneurs can leverage the rules of storytelling and their innate risk tolerance to persuade clients and employees to remain engaged and focused to weather the uncertainty to come.

Many circumstances can affect the mindset of your audience. Have people heard there might be layoffs? You'd better address that elephant. As long as you leave it unattended, nobody will hear your prepared speech. They will be sitting there waiting for you to address it, and every other part of your story will be lost.

Demographics, needs, and attitude—this DNA formula applies whether you're standing in front of a room of people or having a one-on-one meeting. For example, your best salespeople know a prospect's demographic and needs before they get on a call or walk through the door. They know it is part of their job. As a result, they will tweak their pitch for each prospect based on their DNA.

2. IDENTIFY THE ONE THING

Even the best communicators likely only get their audience to remember One Thing from their speech or presentation. The tendency is to ask folks to sit through thing after thing, but the truth is that after a week or a month, they won't remember more than one. For that reason, you need to identify exactly what One Thing you want people to take away, The One Thing you want them to know, think, do, or believe.

Consider the big speeches famous people have given: Martin Luther King's "I Have a Dream," Steve Jobs's "Stay Hungry. Stay Foolish," even Donald Trump's "American Carnage." Whether or not the speakers intended to, these speeches became known for their One Thing. If we think in terms of a fairy tale, The One Thing is the moral to the story. It's your job to decide in advance what you want that to be.

When working with clients on a story, I use the Hansel and

Gretel fairy tale as a metaphor, specifically the part where the brother and sister venture into the woods and leave bread-crumbs on the ground so they can find their way back out (Figure 4.1). In terms of storytelling, however, the breadcrumbs are not for you to find your way back but for the listener to follow your thought process, data points, or insights. The breadcrumbs are the morsels of information, metrics, customer insights, or constructive feedback. They are the clues you lay out to bring your audience to the outcome you've determined ahead of time, The One Thing you want them to know, think, do, or believe.

Figure 4.1. Lead them to The One Thing

The One Thing is at the heart of all storytelling, whether it's a speech, presentation, conversation, or interview. By starting with The One Thing in mind, you can lay out the points that allow your audience to follow your thinking and end up at the conclusion you want, all while thinking it was their idea. This is the art of persuasion.

Whatever the story and whoever the audience, ask yourself,

"What is The One Thing I want my audience to take away from this conversation?" And yes, keep it to *one* to effect change.

If you understand your audience's DNA and your desired goal, you have the foundation of a compelling and engaging story.

TURBULENCE ALERT

I worked with a large organization comprised of business professionals, technologists, academics, and scientists. They had a crucial review meeting to ensure continued funding, and they were excited to share reams of information. However, despite all the impressive data, KPIs, and technology, their story did not have The One Thing. The narrative began as six individual stories, some short, some not so short. Although each might have stood on its own, none embraced a narrative that supported the renewed funding. Because the speaker didn't have one unified moral, the stories read like chapters from different books.

I began to work with the CEO on The One Thing. Their first instinct was for the audience to leave thinking, "We should renew our funding for this company." Over time, the CEO became bolder with The One thing and decided they wanted their audience to conclude, "We should give this company even more than they are asking for." This One Thing informed the story by focusing on not just successes to date but the innovative and exciting opportunities additional funding would create. What started as several stories about goals achieved and past successes became one story about how a unified team enabled those successes and set the organization up for a bolder, more dynamic future.

3. EDIT YOUR STORY

"If I had more time, I would have written you a shorter letter" is a variation on a quote that has been attributed to diverse writers, from Cicero to Mark Twain. Whoever said it, the meaning is the same: we need to edit to keep our message clear and concise.

After you understand your audience DNA and identify your One Thing, you can decide what information your audience needs to hear and in what order they need to hear it so that they can arrive at The One Thing when that conversation, speech, or email is done.

First, gather all your data. When I say "data," I mean everything from actual data and metrics to examples, milestones, events, and even testimonials. Each data point is a breadcrumb or morsel of information that can help a listener follow your path to The One Thing. With everything on the table, you can edit using The One Thing as your guide.

Here's an editing tool I use with my clients. Write your One Thing on a Post-it note and stick it on the wall. Then write every other data point, or breadcrumb, on its own sticky note and post them around your One Thing.

Then go through each breadcrumb and ask yourself, "Does this support The One Thing?" If not, it comes off the wall and doesn't go into the story. It doesn't mean the things eliminated are not important or meaningful; it just means they don't belong in *this* narrative. To include them might send the listener on a tangent that takes them off the path and ultimately causes them to miss your One Thing.

After you sift through your ideas, take each breadcrumb and

put them in a logical order. Ask yourself, "What do they need to hear first? Is this easy to follow? Do any one of these points look out of place?" Working through this process increases the likelihood your listener will arrive at your One Thing.

Streamlining Strategies

In crafting your story and determining what information needs to be shared, you can run into several common pitfalls. Here are some strategies for avoiding those pitfalls so you lead people directly to your One Thing.

Don't Leave Too Many Breadcrumbs

The most common mistake while editing is TMI. When you lay out too many breadcrumbs, you leave people stuffed. They cannot digest one more piece of information, so they tune out, daydream, or walk out. You may have taken three years to digest this information, and now you're asking people to digest it in thirty minutes. That's not going to happen.

Make Sure You Leave Enough Breadcrumbs

Some people swing to the other side and overedit, offering too little information. If there are not enough breadcrumbs, people get lost. If they aren't able to follow your thought process, they can't come to the conclusion to which you're trying to lead them. You have to make sure your narrative isn't missing morsels of information. Otherwise, it's like sitting through a movie that's had four writers and three editors and no vision. It makes no sense, gets 35 percent on Rotten Tomatoes, and leaves the audience thinking, "That sucked."

Avoid Tangents

The next challenge is making sure the breadcrumbs don't go off on tangents. In your storytelling, it's easy to fill in color in one particular area. However, if you add something because *you* think it's interesting or impressive but it has nothing to do with supporting your One Thing, you'll send the audience off on a tangent and away from your goal. Once they get off track, it's difficult to get them back to your original narrative.

4. SCRIPT YOUR STORY

Once you have the data points and know the order in which you need to share them, it's time to script the story. The goal is not to memorize your words. I believe in remembering rather than memorizing your story. However, writing out a script ensures you have the right words while being able to remain engaged and present.

We discussed the power of words in Chapter 2. They can evoke enthusiasm or quell fears. The wrong word can stoke anxieties or even send the stock market crashing, as evidenced by Tesla's 10 percent drop in 2020, after Elon Musk tweeted that his company's stock price was "too high." Choose your words to support your story, and ensure they are painting the right picture for your audience.

When scripting your story, you want to consider the three Rs: real, relevant, relatable.

Make It Real

First, for a business story to be compelling it must be real. An audience will eventually sniff out a boaster, bullshitter, or spin doctor. A "planted story" crafted for the occasion always has an artificial vibe. Such stories fall flat and can undermine your credibility.

It's always more powerful to use your own stories rather than someone else's. There are times when a colleague's story might be useful. I have used client stories in this book to add context to topics discussed. However, they are stories in which I played a part, and I stated that up front. As you use real stories, remember to give credit where credit is due.

Make It Relevant

If your story is only relevant to you, keep it to yourself. By focusing on your audience's DNA and your One Thing, you should be able to keep your story relevant to *them* and increase the likelihood you will lead them to the desired end.

Have you ever sat through someone's vacation photos? Flipping through them is great when you know people in the pictures. If you don't, it's the biggest yawn. Why? If you know people in the photos, then the stories feel relevant to you.

Brands rarely mention their competition in their advertising stories—not because they are not relevant to the consumers' decision making, but because they are not relevant to the brand narrative. Whenever they do make a mention, it is simply to highlight the way in which they are better, faster, cheaper than the competition. The narrative remains relevant to the listener and consistent with their story.

If you don't see how your story or anecdote connects or is relevant to your audience, they won't either.

Make It Relatable

Making a story relatable involves several factors, including word choice and phrasing. Knowing your audience and their needs will help you choose the examples and wording that will be most relatable to your listeners.

I've seen smart leaders try to be funny to loosen up the energy in the room. This is an opportunity for a big miss if their idea of funny and the listeners' idea of funny are not aligned. If you know your audience well and you know they can relate, go for it. Otherwise, your idea of funny may get you and the organization in hot water.

Telling a story to which most of your audience can't relate or connect is worse than telling no story at all. If you've learned your audience's DNA, then you will be better able to shape stories that are truly relatable. Craft a version where the listener can connect with something and find some point of common ground. If they can see themselves in your story, you've got 'em.

5. DELIVER YOUR STORY

The final element of the formula involves delivery. Compelling stories require credible storytellers. How you tell your story must be rooted in your presence, your confidence, and your language of conviction. Since we spent the entire previous chapter examining how leaders can build credibility through their presence and confidence, we're going to focus now on how storytelling can convey credibility through the *language of conviction.*

If you tell a story you don't believe in or agree with, the person hearing the story will sense your lack of conviction. You will signal it in your tone, energy, and body language.

You'll also signal it in the telling because conviction has a language that involves precise word choices. There is a difference between "I think" and "I will." There's a difference between "We're hoping to…" and "Our forecasting shows…" You may be planning to do something, but it doesn't mean you're going to. Use the language of conviction to support your credibility and ensure the listener will follow your breadcrumbs.

The very word *conviction* conveys the need for our beliefs, ideas, and opinions to be fixed and firm. How can we convince others if we are not convinced? If we are in any way unsure or insecure, the language of conviction will elude us.

As a leader, you will occasionally lack certainty or endeavor to clarify a decision or direction. However, when communicating with others, we are better off saying, "I'm still working on the solution" or "I don't have all the answers at the moment, but I will follow up with you within the week," rather than using words like "hoping" or "trying." Investors at a pitch meeting want to know you have conviction about your company, your team, and your vision. In a time of crisis, your team wants to know you have conviction about how to move forward. Board members must always have conviction in your leadership. All of these are informed and communicated through your language of conviction.

TURBULENCE ALERT

I was recently writing a blog post and I caught myself. I was about to write "I feel that communication is…" Suddenly, I realized I had fallen into the language hole that so many people fall into every day, sometimes several times a day. I stopped myself, hit the backspace key, and simply typed "Communication is…"

People commonly use terms such as "I feel" or "I would like" to state their opinions. The truth is, however, doing so puts the ideas and opinions that follow in the context of an emotion, not a fact. By saying "I feel…," I was trying to soften or preface my opinion. However, doing so frames my words as potentially shifting feeling rather than a firm statement. The seeming lack of conviction in the statement weakens my credibility and, by extension, the value of my message. By simply stating "Communication is…," I show my point of view with conviction and certainty.

SLOW DOWN TO SPEED UP

Every media interview, every meeting, every pitch is an opportunity to craft a story that best serves you, your team, and your organization. Not leveraging the storytelling tool means you're missing opportunities to persuade listeners to buy your product, agree with your plan, or trust your leadership. Yes, this means slowing down to identify the audience's DNA, your One Thing, and your story arc. But doing so will streamline and speed up buy-in, engagement, visibility, and by extension, growth.

Another place to leverage storytelling is in your job descriptions so you can land the talent that's the best fit for your organization. That's where we're going next.

TURBULENCE TOOLKIT

Assess

- Am I having a challenge getting buy-in?
- Are we meeting our conversion goals in sales?
- Do I receive insightful questions after a presentation or pitch?
- Do I start preparing for a presentation, speech, or big meeting by opening PowerPoint?
- Am I clear about the goal (The One Thing) I want to achieve in the meeting, conversation, or presentation?
- Do I craft stories (messages) for myself or for them?
- Did I cram the night before for exams, and do I replicate that at work?
- Can I list all the stories within my organization?
- Do I see myself as a strong storyteller?

Be Intentional

- Slow down and figure out what stories you need to tell and who needs to hear them.
- Make sure you have determined your One Thing beforehand.
- Figure out the right language and tone for expressing your One Thing and reaching your audience.
- Figure out the best way to tell your story: written memo, video message, company town hall or staff meeting, and so on.
- Encourage storytelling as a skill for leadership development.
- Have conviction about your story. People can smell bullshit.
- Road test your story. One of the great things about stories is that you can constantly edit them to make them better. The more you practice an elevator pitch, the more you're going to hone in on the valuable elements. You'll learn what people gravitate toward and

what they ask questions about. The same is true of a sales pitch. The more you road test it, the more you say it out loud, the more you can perfect the story.

Pick One Thing

- Vision story
- Value story
- Pitch story
- Audience DNA
- The One Thing
- Editing your story
- Scripting your story
- The three Rs
- Language of conviction

Dig Deeper

- *The Art of Rhetoric* by Aristotle
- *Brain Rules: 12 Principles for Surviving and Thriving at Work, Home, and School* by John Medina
- *Made to Stick: Why Some Ideas Survive and Others Die* by Chip Heath and Dan Heath
- The Power of Words: storyarts.org
- *Stories That Stick: How Storytelling Can Captivate Customers, Influence Audiences, and Transform Your Business* by Kindra Hall

CHAPTER 5

TALENT

LEVERAGE THE LAWS OF ATTRACTION

"Acquiring the right talent is the most important key to growth. Hiring was—and still is—the most important thing we do."

—MARC BENIOFF

If you've engaged in online dating, then you know a little something about seeking to attract the right person. You create a profile that will put you in the best light for any prospective dates. You choose photos that make you look good, and you write descriptions that will garner winks or likes or whatever positive response that particular app uses.

When some people create profiles, however, they don't use the most up-to-date photos, and they sometimes polish their descriptions a little too much. They may end up on a date or, worse, in a relationship that is not a good match.

In the dating world, many people are fine with a temporary, short-term fling, but no one wants that in the working world. We want to build lasting relationships with employees. Yet many organizations go looking for love in all the wrong places, slap together a job description that makes promises they can't keep, or don't look beyond the profile photo before swiping left.

People—what I call "talent" here—are the number one line item on any company's P&L, yet this is where most leaders spend the least amount of resources hiring, supporting, improving, and innovating. Growing organizations are often slow to invest in a head of HR, a hiring manager, or even an outsourced recruiter. If talent is your biggest investment, why not have a hiring expert on your team? I look forward to the day when every C-suite has a CHRO. However, whether you have such an expert on your team, you'll want to become one yourself to ensure you attract the right talent. After all, your people are the key to helping you execute your vision, and vision without execution is hallucination.

To attract the right people for each role in the company, we have to be transparent about who we are as an organization, what we stand for, and what potential employees can expect from us and the role. We also need to ensure the process is not all about us. It's about a mutual decision regarding that person's alignment with our company and the role.

When a company grows rapidly, it's common to hire quickly. The old adage of "Be slow to hire, and quick to fire" goes out the window when things need to get done. Leaders start hiring by proximity. Who's available? Who can start on Monday? Who has a friend who knows marketing? We're in such a hurry to put someone in the seat that we don't take time to make sure it's the right body in the right seat.

"VISION WITHOUT EXECUTION IS HALLUCINATION."

Even if we take the time to post a job and conduct multiple interviews, we may not slow down long enough to ensure we are looking in the right places, attracting the right candidates, interviewing effectively, and setting up new hires for success. Although these quick hires are done to save time, they actually cost time and money in the long run.

Hiring quickly and/or poorly creates challenges for ourselves and our organizations that have far-reaching implications. The daily stress and strain of trying to make a bad hire work effectively is challenging enough. When the employee eventually quits or gets fired, there's extra paperwork for HR, messy client transfers, and then the organization must go through the hiring and training process all over again. Employee Benefit News reported in 2017 that turnover can cost employers 33 percent of an employee's annual salary due to the cost of hiring a replacement.[19] Conclusion: hiring with intention is one of the best investments your company can make.

Doing talent acquisition right will probably take more time than you want to give it, but putting in the work to leverage effective communication tools and strategies up front will enable you to be more efficient in your hiring. Ultimately, you'll minimize turbulence caused by the employee disengagement and turnover that would have resulted from rushing through it.

This chapter will help you craft the right job description, attract the right talent, and onboard people with intention and consistency.

---

19   Nick Otto, "Avoidable Turnover Costing Employers Big," Employee Benefit News, August 9, 2017, https://www.benefitnews.com/news/avoidable-turnover-costing-employers-big?brief=00000152-14a7-d1cc-a5fa-7cffccf00000&utm_content=socialflow&utm_campaign=ebnmagazine&utm_source=twitter&utm_medium=social.

CANDIDATE BLUEPRINT

Attracting the best hire takes time. That is why effective leaders leverage HR professionals to create, lead, and refine a clear and scalable process. Taking time allows you to follow Wayne Gretzky's observation and hire for where the role and organization are going, not where they are or have been.

It never ceases to surprise me how many growing organizations hire by proximity. They don't execute a full talent search, even when hiring for a leadership position. Instead, they put the word out through their network or with their connections on LinkedIn and hire from that pool. You may still end up finding an ideal candidate that way, but if you didn't go out and look, how will you know they were the best?

Slowing down also ensures you are clear about what you need for the role and what potential employees need to know during the hiring process. When articulating what you need, it is helpful to think beyond the day-to-day tasks or even previous roles held. Skills are obviously important; however, it's equally important to look for character qualities, mindset, diversity of perspective, and value alignment—and often more so. In taking the time to prepare your candidate blueprint, you ensure you truly attract the right individuals for your organization and culture.

ATTRACT FOR CULTURE

In the past ten years, there has been a great deal written and discussed about culture. More and more companies are intentionally focusing on their company culture, taking note of how it helps or hurts their organization. It's important to remember that whether or not you have been intentional about crafting your culture, you do have one. It may not be the one you want, but you have one. That culture, whatever it is at the time of hiring, is what you need to share with potential employees. Not being honest about it is like posting an old photo on Match.com: it will eventually be revealed as a lie.

You might have what I call a "pants-on-fire" work environment, where people are constantly fifteen minutes late to meetings because there are never enough hours in a day. Or you might have a highly competitive, kill-what-you-eat culture. If that is truly the culture you have, that's fine; just be up front about it. You don't want to attract someone who's looking for social events on Friday afternoon and yoga and meditation on Monday morning.

Attract the people who see themselves aligning with your culture. As shown in this chapter's In Their Words sidebar, being aligned in culture is a big factor in both recruitment and retention. You waste potential employees' time—not to mention your team's time and money—in attracting, vetting, and hiring people who will be uncomfortable in the culture and disengage. No matter how talented, no matter what their skillset, there will always be turbulence with that person in that role because they are not right for your culture. If you are honest and no one is attracted to your organization (I've seen that happen more often than you'd think), don't then lie about it or photoshop it to entice talent. Instead, shift your culture. This is a much harder lift but one more and more organizations will have to make to attract the talent of the future.

REDEFINE "FIT"

Attracting for culture is not the same as looking for "fit." Fit is rigid. It implies that only a certain person or skillset will work in a given position. Think of a garden: rather than trying to find a plant that fits in a certain-sized hole, find the right plant and then dig the hole to make that plant part of your garden. Hiring for fit instead of finding the right person can be costly and create all kinds of turbulence.

In a sense, we need to stop thinking about fit. Often, a "good fit" means "They should be like me" or "I'll like working with them." It is natural to have an internal dialogue about "liking" someone as we look for and interview candidates. However, if we use "liking" as the definition of fit, we do a disservice to the candidates, the organization, and ourselves. When we take the time to redefine the many shapes and sizes that fit, we open up the door to some valuable team members. Not unlike a pair of skinny jeans, it just may take a bit of time for them to fit like a glove.

A colleague of mine uses a Hiring Matrix (based on a traditional Decision Matrix) for his organization, which ensures he compares apples to apples, looks and listens for alignment, and avoids the natural tendency to put all the weight on gut feelings. This type of matrix can help you ensure you look and listen for certain qualities and potential red flags when evaluating candidates.

The categories in a Hiring Matrix will vary widely depending on the organization and position. For example, my Hiring Matrix might include "comfortable and articulate on the phone," "happy working daily in the details," and "confident enough to hold me accountable." Another company's matrix might include "high risk tolerance," "techy savvy," and "can hold their own in contentious meetings." By identifying these qualities before the interviewing process begins, if you have two qualified candidates, you have a tool to objectively evaluate based not on "fit" but on things like culture, alignment, and traits you define well in advance.

By redefining fit—rather, by not thinking of it as fit at all—you move away from trying to hire for a rigid box. Although many people think of laws as rigid, they actually have boundaries within which there is room to maneuver. By hiring according to the following laws of attraction instead of fit, you can find the best candidates and ensure they are in the right roles.

IN THEIR OWN WORDS: TAYLOR

When Taylor started the interview process with Scribe Media, she was simultaneously interviewing with another company. She was initially more excited about the other opportunity, but that changed as the interviewing and hiring process went on, as she explains here:

> I knew that I wanted to pursue more marketing-based positions, and I knew I didn't want to live in Los Angeles. I had been looking in other cities that had growing industries and were really booming. I typed in marketing and [the job at Scribe] was one of the first three roles that popped up.
>
> I clicked on it just because of the job description. There were several things that really caught my eye and made me apply. The first one was the fact that they included a hidden line in the application. That was crazy smart because they need people who have attention to detail, and anybody who didn't catch that line was automatically weeded out. When I read that question, it showed me that they had that same value. I had found my people.

One of the things Taylor appreciated was that Scribe was up front about their culture.

They really emphasized that this is a place where people work really hard, but they also care about the people they work with. They emphasized that if you want an environment where you can show up and work with people who are driven and who want to be successful and support this company, this is the place for you. But if you are intimidated by that, then don't apply.

They also included a link to what they call the Culture Bible. It's a public document that's on the website. What really attracted me was the fact that people were the number one value, whether it's the Scribe Tribe members or their authors. I spent a very long time reading through that before I even applied because it was just so different and refreshing.

One of my favorite parts in the document is, "Bathrooms are for going to the bathroom, but not for crying. If you need to cry, do it in the office with people who care about you." I read that and thought, "I've cried in the bathroom at my old jobs. I've cried in stairwells." I used to hide all the struggles that I was facing at my last job. And here it was so evident that they wanted to support not only your work but you as a person.

So I applied. They emailed me back within a few hours and invited me to the next round. I had to record video responses to a few questions about marketing.

One of the things I really appreciated throughout this entire process was that they were very good at communicating with me. I was never guessing about when I was going to hear back. They always had an automatic response stating you would hear back within a certain time frame. And they always followed through with that commitment. They had clear expectations.

The next round was with the Head of People. I went

into the interview prepared to answer questions about the role and my skillset and my past experience, but the interview wasn't specific to my work experience. He asked me to just tell him my story. Then we talked about the Scribe culture. He was trying to see if I would be a good fit for Scribe. It also allowed me to see if Scribe would be a good fit for me.

During the next interview, the Head of Marketing started the interview with, "So what questions do you have for me?" Almost the entire interview was spent by me asking him questions, which was very unique.

I was actually interviewing for another job at the same time, and the contrast between my experience interviewing at that job and with Scribe solidified the fact that I wanted to work for Scribe. I had been very excited about the other position; it sounded like a great job at a great company. However, as I went through their interview process, I got progressively less excited about it.

My first interview was over the phone; it was a typical interview, talking about my past experience. She had me submit some samples of work that I had done over the past few years. I sent that in, and then I never heard back. I had to follow up again to ensure that she received it, and then she did respond and invited me to come in for an in-person interview. It turned out that they were hiring for three roles in one and none matched the job description they had posted. I didn't get a sense of what it was like to work there at all. I had no idea, except that they were unhappy and it sounded like they were very disorganized.

Ultimately, Scribe offered Taylor the marketing position, and she accepted.

Before my start date, they scheduled a pre-onboarding so we could start setting up HR elements. The official process lasted about a week and I was on onboarded with two other new employees. Throughout the onboarding process, they asked us questions about how we were feeling and what we thought of the job requirements; they also asked whether we had any concerns. It was very therapeutic, which is a weird word for onboarding, but it made me feel very comfortable. They bought us lunch the first day, and the rest of the week was spent primarily with my "direct support"—my boss. Scribe's choice to call bosses "direct supports" is another way they set the tone for the work environment. He walked me through Scribe's marketing philosophies, the kind of authors we work with, and why we do what we do. The focus was more on outcomes than on process.

I did get a chance to meet individually with other team members; they walked me through their roles, explained how I would support them, and what my initial responsibilities would be. We got an hour-long Q&A session with Scribe's CEO and co-founders, which was awesome. And it was no holds barred. We could ask whatever we wanted, and they were 100 percent honest. It seemed like they respected the hard questions even more because I was willing to ask them.

Taylor's story highlights a well-thought-out and -executed hiring and onboarding process. Yes, creating the videos and having multiple meetings with leadership takes time, but the rewards are evident in how Taylor feels about her job and the organization.

LAWS OF ATTRACTION

If hiring is like dating, then as a leader you want to ensure you attract the right person, that you are creative about where to find them, and that they feel sure yours is the right organization for them. The following four laws can help you do just that.

LAW 1: JOB DESCRIPTIONS ARE A STORY

Job descriptions are the first chapter of your organization's value story. They will determine who you attract and who self-selects out.

Start from Scratch

Think back to the last time you had to hire someone to fill a role. Did you pull up the job description that you used the previous time you had to hire somebody? Chances are, the answer is yes. You may have tweaked it to add new tasks or responsibilities, but on the whole, it was probably the same. We rarely want to start with a blank sheet of paper when we're putting together a job description, so we usually recycle what we've already used.

In any organization, but especially a rapidly growing one, that old job description is most likely out of date. The company, the culture, and the role itself have probably evolved. You now have a much better understanding of what makes someone successful in that role, and you are better able to articulate the qualities and skillsets that will make someone successful in it.

Don't simply go back to a file and pull out an old description. Instead, start from where you are today and think about where the company is heading. If your organization is growing rapidly, even that new job description will be nearly out of date by the time you actually hire someone. As with the company vision, you want to think about where this individual needs to be in eighteen to twenty-four months. You don't want to hire someone who is great for the role today but isn't going to scale with the role over time. They don't need all the skills today, but they should be coachable and have the qualities to grow with the team and the organization.

Frame Your Story

Even if we do start with a blank sheet of paper instead of an old description, our tendency is to break down a job description into tasks and requirements. The problem is that filling a role is not simply about the tasks to be done.

A traditional job description might list responsibilities like "Work closely with marketing, sales, and customer success teams" or "Analyze and interpret financial data." Someone might be able to check off those tasks, but that doesn't mean they're good at them. "Work closely" is vague. Does this require a proactive, extroverted, or collaborative individual? What qualities are required of the hire that will ensure they are good at working closely with marketing, sales, and customer service? Those qualities might be different than if they work closely with IT, for instance, or finance or new hires versus board members. Identify and attract people who have, and self-identify as having, the abilities needed to be successful in the job—not someone who can merely tick off a task.

If a job description is a story, then crafting it follows the same formula presented in Chapter 4:

1. Consider the DNA (demographics, needs, attitude) of your audience—your potential candidates.
2. Identify The One Thing—the most important quality you're looking for, whether it's the ability to work productively from home or someone who will grow and thrive in your culture.
3. Edit your job description so that you lead the right potential candidates to your One Thing and self-select out as necessary.
4. Script your story. Take time to identify the words and

phrases that paint an accurate picture of your culture so that the people you seek opt in and apply or simply self-select out.
5. Deliver your story. Delivery in a job description context not only involves posting on the right outlets. It also includes involving the right people in the interview process.

A favorite example of mine comes from the MIT Media Lab. When the founder, architect Nicholas Negroponte, was looking to find the right leader for his new endeavor, he added the word *misfit* to the first line of the posting. What a rich word. Some people may hate being described as a misfit, but those who identify as such would surely be drawn to that word in a job description. It is so telling about not just the type of person they were seeking but also the type of culture and organization they were building.

Identify Their Default Setting

One of the most common challenges I see in rapidly growing organizations is that they really need two people but have the resources to hire only one, so they create one role and try to shoehorn someone into it. What they don't realize is that the skills, qualities, and default work mode needed to be successful in one job are often quite different from those needed in another, and those two skillsets may not live in the same person.

TURBULENCE ALERT

A client was recently looking for a junior hire to manage both graphic design and the details of the CRM. That's a bit of a unicorn. In general, there are people who usually think in broad strokes, viewing the world from 10,000 feet up, and those whose gift is swimming in the details. Those two skillsets—having a broad vision and the ability to see the minutiae to make it work—don't usually exist in one person. It doesn't mean they *can't* do it. It simply means they may not do it at the level needed. My client determined that he was positioned for only one new hire and decided to hire for the one strength that would add the greatest value in the short term, the CRM. He knew the individual might need added support and training for other tasks and that down the line he would hire a graphic designer.

After ten years working as a communications consultant, I've observed that an individual's default method of processing information informs so much of their workplace value. Some people are methodical thinkers. Some have to process thoughts out loud. Some can see the black grain of sand in a sea of white, and some see the coastline, not just a beach. It's not a matter of right or wrong, good or bad. It just is.

When you're outlining needed qualities and skills in the job description, slow down to ensure they are not diametrically opposite. If you see many qualities that seemingly require someone to work at both ends of the spectrum, chances are, you're going to have a hard time finding those qualities in the same person.

If your job description is not realistic for one person, then you're setting a new hire up for failure. You end up with turbulence on many levels: the new hire is unhappy, the boss is stressed because the person isn't doing what's needed, the team experiences delays because the person isn't contributing as expected, and the company will lose money when the person finally quits and another person has to be found to fill the role.

Don't Hire the Anti-Ex

In the dating world, when we break up with someone, we often look for a person who is the opposite of whatever qualities we believe led to the breakup. For example, if your ex was a homebody and you are tired of binge-watching Netflix, you might look for someone who is outgoing and social. However, although the new person might be highly social, they could have other red flags we didn't see because we were so focused on finding the anti-ex.

Something similar often happens in organizations. They let someone go because they weren't a good "fit," and then they create a job description designed to avoid the qualities in the last person that didn't work. You can often find wording in a job description that seems to highlight this tendency. Sometimes it shows up in qualifying statements that hint at what was missing. For example, rather than simply stating that the person must have great presentation skills, the post might add the qualifier "including *large group* and conference settings" because the last person was great one-on-one but not comfortable in large groups of strangers. This tendency also shows up in the use of descriptors. Saying the new hire must be able to "craft *creative* communications"—as opposed to *internal* communications or *compelling* communications—may stem from the last person's writing, which was likely not "creative," as the company defines it.

Avoiding the ex's qualities may be important, and it's healthy to constantly iterate a job description as you gain greater understanding of the role or as the organization grows. However, focusing on what you don't want and dismissing new red flags is not the way to attract the right person for the role.

Instead, start from scratch. Be very clear on what you need so potential applicants will understand and either apply or self-select out. If you focus on being clear about what you *don't* want, the potential applicant may still not be clear about what you *do* want.

The structure of one client's organization was such that working remotely was required, but a previous employee had a challenge with this aspect of the job. The real issue was that the person hated her job; however, my client kept focusing on the problems this individual had related to working remotely. When the client began looking for a new hire, she put in the job description, "Comfortable working remotely." No one will admit they are uncomfortable working remotely, so I suggested she might reword it to be more precise, something like "Most effective working remotely" or "Engaged when working remotely." My client needed to word the job description based on what she needed from the new person in the role—not what wasn't working with the last person.

This situation also shows why word choice is so important. Saying "Comfortable working from home" is different than "Most efficient working from home" or "Productive working from home." "Prefer working from home" doesn't capture it either because some people might prefer it simply because they don't like to commute or enjoy working in pajamas, but that doesn't mean they will be most productive. Making sure you refine your word choice helps people identify as precisely as possible with what you're looking for.

As a role evolves, you can strengthen your ability as a hiring expert by keeping notes on new skills or qualities that the role requires. Observe the qualities of an employee that makes them more successful at their job or, conversely, lead to struggle. The qualities, skills, and disposition needed for roles change as the company changes over time.

TURBULENCE ALERT

Two of my clients, co-owners of a company, needed to fill a role quickly, so they looked to Theresa, a vendor with whom they had already done a lot of business. They trusted Theresa and they all got along, so they hired her.

What my clients didn't do was sit down to figure out the value a new hire should bring to the organization. By extension, they had not articulated the qualities and skills needed to help them grow their business. They didn't define clearly where and how they needed to support the company's growth. They didn't think about the qualities or the "default work setting" this individual needed to have. They also didn't post a job description or even put the word out through their networks. They simply hired the individual they already knew and felt was a good "fit."

If they had taken time up front to think about the role and define the skills, qualities, and experience needed, the resulting job description would not have described Theresa. In fact, Theresa likely wouldn't have taken the job because she would have self-selected out. Big shock—she ended up leaving after six months. In that time, she had already caused quite a bit of turbulence.

After Theresa left, my clients were back in the same place of needing to hire someone. This time, we outlined *what* they needed, not *who*: What were the tasks they needed to get off their plate? What was falling through the cracks? What skills and qualities would it take to be good at those tasks? We looked for keywords that would stand out to the right candidates, like "minutiae," "happiest behind a computer," and "loves an Excel spreadsheet."

What my clients realized is that they needed someone who was able to spend the day in the details and had a gift for creating and managing processes, giving them the bandwidth to focus elsewhere. Theresa was great at business development and client relations, but so were my clients. They needed someone who understood their industry but could update and manage the back-end processes, not the front-end interactions. They had tasked Theresa with doing this, but like one of those shopping carts that always swerves left, she would start building a back-end process and then inevitably end up talking to clients on the front end. She was never going to be good at what they needed her to be great at because that was not her zone of genius.

In addition to framing your job description with your audience in mind, you need to attract them with intention.

LAW 2: ATTRACT WITH INTENTION

Advertisers spend millions finding how and where to reach their target audience. The options are endless—TV, streaming services, podcasts, social media, billboards in Times Square. They micro-target to the time of day and day of the week. How often do we follow this example when we are looking to find the right talent? We tend to go to the same job boards, the same social networks, and the same events, when we should take a cue from advertisers.

Start by thinking about *where* you will find the people who would be perfect for the role. You want to find the pool that has the majority of people who are in that space or at the level you're seeking. If your tech company wants to increase diversity, you might advertise at Howard University rather than Stanford. If you're looking for someone with an entrepreneurial mindset, you could post on a co-founder meet-up rather than a corporate job board. Different positions may require posting in different places depending on what you're seeking.

The answer may be within your organization. Provided you are clear about the skills and qualities required for the job, an effective internal hire can be ideal. Hiring internally is faster, you hire a known quantity, and no onboarding is needed. It is also less expensive to hire and train from within (research shows external hires are 61 percent more likely to be fired than internal hires[20]), not to mention employee morale and engagement can increase if people know you look internally first. Be aware there may be diamonds in the rough in your organization. Not everyone is great at self-promotion. Go looking for them and invite them to self-select in.

That said, hiring internally might not be the right step for every hire or every role, and it's certainly not the best way to go simply because it feels easiest. Your goal is to find the *best* person for the job. That may require that you look outside your current workforce. Although there are benefits to hiring internally, there are also proven benefits to hiring externally, from providing fresh perspective to adding new skillsets, qualities, and experience.

---

20   Matthew Bidwell, "Paying More to Get Less: The Effects of External Hiring versus Internal Mobility," Administrative Quarterly 56, no. 3 (2011): 369–407, https://doi.org/10.1177/0001839211433562.

Whether you look internally or externally, attracting the right talent is like any other marketing endeavor. You need to know your audience. Are you looking for someone who's on Snapchat or Instagram or LinkedIn? Do they read *The New York Times* or *The Onion*? And considering the type of person you want to attract, what platform are they most likely to use for job searching? You may have to ask others where to post. There may be an ideal place that you have never thought of or heard about.

I'm on the board of a new and growing nonprofit that was looking for its first Development Director (nonprofit speak for a fundraiser). They posted on their Facebook feed and on their website with no luck. However, as soon as they posted it on the AFP (Association for Fundraising Professionals) website, they attracted two incredible candidates and made an amazing hire.

Getting out of the rut is especially important if you are looking to build diversity within your organization. Not everyone watches the same channel or shops at the same store. Get out of the well-worn path and try new avenues for your candidate search.

It's not unlike dating. If you are looking for love in all the wrong places, you'll end up with turbulence in the relationship. Try to identify places that might have a concentration of more likely candidates.

LAW 3: INTERVIEWING IS ALCHEMY

Interviews are invaluable, but they also involve taking employees in the organization away from their work to help evaluate every single candidate. That adds up to a lot of hours and thus a lot of money. For that reason, ensure you get the most out of the interview process. Being intentional in your interviews will not only net you a better hire; it will also likely net you more dollars.

Don't Get the Right Answer to the Wrong Question

We often interview from a set of standard questions. Some people go online and find questions that someone else has created, or they stumble on blog posts for "Best Interview Questions of the Year," or they look for tools and resources to help craft better questions.

At the end of the day, however, if you focus on what *you* are looking for in a new hire, the qualities and skills needed for someone to be successful should inform your questions. For instance, let's say that you need to find a candidate who is proactive, with excellent attention to detail. During the interview, make sure your questions lead to answers that help you determine whether a candidate has those qualities.

The challenge here is that you can rarely ask these questions directly, because people will tell you what you want to hear. We all do it. It's how we are wired. What interviewee is going to admit, "You know, I have terrible attention for detail" or "I am not proactive at all"? Take the time to craft questions that get you the information you need, ones that will help you assess if the candidate has the skills and qualities you're looking for without asking for it point blank.

One of the first things you learn in qualitative marketing is to triangulate around the question you need answered. Crafting several versions of the same question using different keywords or describing a different scenario can elicit answers that reveal whether the candidate is aligned with the job's requirements.

Leverage active listening and note whether the person gives the same essential answer or if it changes when the questions is worded differently.

For example, here are three versions of the same question related to a person's approach to negative feedback:[21]

- Tell me about a time when you received negative feedback from your boss.
- Are you motivated or demotivated by negative feedback?
- If you were to give yourself constructive feedback, what would it be?

Here are three ways of asking about a person's decision-making process:

- How do you weigh pros and cons before making a decision?
- What is your typical process for decision making?
- What is your process for decision making under pressure?

It takes time to craft the right questions. Start with what you really want to learn. In other words, what are you assessing? Even after you create one list, you may not be able to recycle the same questions in every interview regardless of the role. Drafting new questions means more work; I get it. But the turbulence avoided and the money saved by making the right hire are worth it.

---

21 For information on questionnaire design, see Pew Research Center, "Questionnaire Design," Pew Research Centers: Methods, n.d., https://www.pewresearch.org/methods/u-s-survey-research/questionnaire-design/. The first question in each list comes from this article.

Interviewers

We don't often think about the diversity of perspectives and skills of those who interview candidates. We default to the potential candidate's new boss and the head of HR, along with a coworker or two. These are important and relevant people to include, but who else should be part of the interview process? If you are looking for a collaborator, ensure a collaborator interviews them. If you need someone who is comfortable speaking up, have them interviewed by a highly talkative employee. If they get a word in edgewise, they have communicated to you they are comfortable speaking up.

Again, you have to slow down. Be intentional about what information you want to gather from the interview and which team member(s) might aid in doing so.

Communication is as much about listening as it is about talking. When you take time to make sure you're asking the right questions, it means you're listening for the qualities that are important to you. Interviews are not so much about the text or the answers a candidate provides; they're about the subtext or the meaning behind the message. For instance, take note of how detailed the answers are; that will suggest the level of detail the person will use in their work. If someone is being interviewed by a talkative employee and their body language communicates a shrinking back or if they become suddenly quiet, this person might not be comfortable speaking up. Leverage active listening, be present, and ensure the interviewers look out for signals and subtext—not just the answers but all that the candidate communicates, verbal and nonverbal.

LAW 4: ONBOARDING REQUIRES FOLLOW-THROUGH

Taking the time to onboard properly can make an enormous difference in employee retention, productivity, and ultimately, revenue. Yet, in rapid-growth environments, onboarding tends to go by the wayside; according to one study, only 12 percent of employees say their organization does a good job of onboarding.[22] Why? Because it requires thought and intention to determine what onboarding looks like in a company, and leaders often don't make the time to create these systems and ensure every new hire goes through the same process.

To avoid the turbulence of turnover, disengaged employees, or low productivity, it is imperative that leaders build a comprehensive and well-articulated onboarding system that allows new employees to feel welcomed, at ease, and confident from the minute they walk in the door. They need clarity on what is expected. They should know their voice can be heard. You certainly wouldn't want them to feel like lost tourists wandering around a foreign country.

What can you do to ensure that your onboarding process supports the growth of the company instead of causing turbulence? Here are some suggestions.

Make People Feel Welcome

If you want people to feel welcome, you actually have to welcome them. You also have to make sure you welcome every person, every time. If one person is onboarded following the hiring process but someone else isn't, you've already created

---

22   "State of the American Workplace," Gallup, 2017, https://www.gallup.com/workplace/238085/state-american-workplace-report-2017.aspx.

turbulence. You've communicated that one person is more important or somehow more valued than another.

Effective onboarding requires intention and consistency to create an easily replicable process for onboarding new hires. It's important to ensure you carry out this process every time and that the process itself makes people feel welcome. That replicable and scalable system may mean you don't personally welcome everyone on their day one, but you could engage in a different way that works with your schedule, like ensuring you have a new-hires lunch every couple of weeks to talk with them.

The manner in which you make new hires feel welcome depends on your organization's culture. If you have a dog-eat-dog, eat-what-you-kill kind of culture, the way you welcome new hires will be very different than if you have a slower paced, more collaborative culture. Someone doesn't feel welcome simply because they have a desk or know how to set up their Slack account. Those things are helpful and necessary, but they don't make someone feel welcome. That is not effective onboarding.

Welcome means "to receive or accept with pleasure." Work to convey that message in ways that are authentic to your culture; then you'll be headed in the right direction. Welcoming people means making them feel like they are part of the team. It means having a conversation, asking questions, checking in periodically to see how they're adjusting. Taylor's onboarding experience involved all of the above and made her feel comfortable from the beginning.

Onboarding doesn't only happen in the person's first hour on the job. It happens over the first week or even month as you check in periodically to make sure they are quickly and seamlessly becoming part of the team. Your onboarding process should be viewed as an integration, not a "wham-bam, thank you, ma'am" experience.

Set Clear Expectations

After making employees feel welcome, the next step is to set crystal-clear expectations. This should be the most fundamental phase of onboarding, and it's all about clarity and alignment.

Expectation setting falls into several buckets.

Organizational Expectations

As part of the onboarding process, sit down with the new hire and talk to them about your company's values. Hopefully, you already did this in the interviews, job description, and throughout the hiring process. Now you can put a finer point on how the employee can expect to see those values in your culture, in handling problems with a customer, or when there's a disagreement on the team. Help the new employee understand how to navigate waters they've never been in. In setting these kinds of expectations, you're giving the person a map, not of the office but of the whole organization.

TURBULENCE ALERT

One company with which I worked was very clear about its values. They discussed them on the website, in the job description, and in their interviews. One of those values was "Always on top of it," with the idea being that they would always be one step ahead of their clients or the problem. No matter what the situation, they stressed that their employees should always stay on top of it.

A young woman, Maya, was hired by this company. Even though Maya had gone through three rounds of interviews and met five different people in the organization, not one of them put a block of time in their calendar to show up at the door and introduce her to someone who would help her through her onboarding process.

Instead, Maya was greeted by Brandon, whom she'd never met, was led to her desk with a computer, and was given a Post-it note with some log-in info. Then Brandon said, "I'll meet you in the kitchen at lunchtime to see if you have any questions."

From the word go, Maya felt tentative about the organization. How could she feel successful if she had no tools to be successful other than what she brought with her?

At lunch, Maya went to the kitchen and found Brandon, but he couldn't answer any of her questions because he was from HR, not Maya's department. To make matters worse, Maya's boss was out of town and had not communicated that this would be the case. This gave Maya the impression that her boss would likely be too busy or too distracted to be a helpful presence in her work life. She also assumed that she must have a low value to the company if her boss didn't care to be at the office on her first day or make other plans to welcome her.

About ten days later, Maya finally sat down with her boss. As they were going over the to-do list, Maya's boss said, "You're already a day behind."

"But today is Wednesday. This is due Friday," Maya said.

"Yeah, but for us, being on top of it means tasks are completed three days before they're due."

This was not a written rule; it was an expectation—one that had not been communicated to Maya in onboarding (since there was none); neither was it communicated by Brandon or by anyone else she'd had contact with during the ten days she'd worked before meeting with her boss.

Maya understood the company's value of "being on top of it," but she didn't know how that value showed up in the organization or how she was expected to embody it. Expectations like this must be communicated for the success of the individual as well as the team and organization.

To avoid turbulence around expectations, define terms, put expectations in writing, and ask the new hire to rephrase what they heard to ensure you are on the same page.

Individual Expectations

A leader's expectations are primarily concerned with a new hire's performance in the job they were hired to do. However, beyond the tasks, a new hire also needs to understand how to engage and communicate effectively with their leader, how the team works most effectively together, and what tools they need to avoid turbulence.

The way in which the boss communicates these expectations may be as simple as, "If you have a simple problem, put it on Slack. Don't send me an email." Let new employees know how you want to engage with them and how you intend to communicate.

In Chapter 1, I mentioned the DISC assessment and how it can provide useful information for your teams. I recommended that the assessment be used to create individual reports, describing communication preferences. In my own report, the page titled "Ways to Communicate with Monique" says things like, "Provide ideas for implementing action" and "Leave time for relating and socializing." The next page, titled "Ways NOT to Communicate with Monique," says, "Don't leave decisions hanging in the air" and "Don't ramble." Articulating these preferences helps my team know I want to hear solutions from them and that I enjoy some chitchat to begin a meeting. That clarity around expectations helps create smooth workplace dynamics.

I also set expectations around communication channels. My staff knows if a problem is urgent, call me. I will answer if I'm not with a client. The rest of the team has completed their own DISC reports about communication preferences, which means we've had a chance to learn one another's preferred styles.

Doing this up front cuts down on miscommunication, which cuts down on turbulence. It also mitigates the apprehension people feel in their first few months in a new role when they're trying to figure out what's going on. People may have simple questions, but they are important to the employees' success and productivity. It's important to set expectations on how to get those questions answered. Understanding in advance how your boss or team works most efficiently or what creates challenges for them is like being given a map to a minefield.

TURBULENCE ALERT

One of my clients was head of a very large organization. Keshia was well respected in her industry, but it was heavily male dominated and she'd fought tooth and nail to get where she was.

One of the challenges she shared with me is that she had a hard time letting anyone send an email or communication without her double-checking it. She had to make sure everything was buttoned up tight and absolutely perfect, which slowed people down and created a ridiculous amount of work for herself. It also crafted a narrative that she was a micromanager.

Keshia finally reached the point where she realized this wasn't working and she needed to take her hands off and delegate, so she came up with a plan. She told her team they would work together for three months so that they all understood her voice and the way she wanted things done. After three months, Keshia agreed to trust their work and stop asking to review every email. She gave them permission to push back if she asked to see something before it went out, even giving them a script of what to say when she tried to take that last look.

She also started having this conversation with every new employee. If there had been no conversation, new hires probably would have felt micromanaged for those first three months. However, because she did have that conversation, new employees understood what was happening during those three months of close supervision and they felt empowered. They understood Keshia's expectations: "We're going to spend three months working together hand in hand, and then you're on your own. At that point, if I try to stick my finger in the pie, you're invited to push back and tell me to take it the heck out. That's my challenge and I'm working on it." How much confidence would that give a new employee? For Keshia's new hires, quite a bit.

When I worked in the film industry, I worked for one of the firm's managing partners, who had a reputation for being a yeller. As a result, no one worked in his office for longer than three months. One woman lasted only ten days. On the tenth day, she went to lunch and never came back.

The company was growing fast and hiring in a hurry. Through word of mouth, I heard about, interviewed, and got the job within a week. However, nowhere along the line did anyone give me a heads-up about this individual's personality and aggressive style.

As a matter of fact, my first-day "welcome" involved seeing this managing partner kick a box down the hall, yell expletives, and complain about a client. I don't know what I expected but not that. There was no hello from anyone other than the two wonderful receptionists. Oddly, I was not offended by the partner's behavior. I laughed, actually, because he looked ridiculous.

However, while he quickly communicated to me the culture of his office, I was unclear how to ensure I didn't personally ignite that display of temper. I was able to work with this guy, but as evidenced by the fact that they had gone through five people in three months, many people could not.

Given this manager's style, part of the interview process should have involved communicating what he was like and getting clear buy-in from me that I was up for the challenge. The onboarding process should have included a heads-up of his triggers, some tools and tricks to manage eruptions, and maybe a signal book to identify blowups before they happened.

If this guy were open to feedback, in any way coachable, or had any interest in becoming a great leader, he would have known that his presence, energy, and communication style created not just turbulence but tidal waves of turmoil across the organization. Such a leader would have let new employees know up front, "Look, I have a temper. I'm loud and I yell. I'm working on it." Or even "I have no intention of changing. Can you handle it?"

New hires need a roadmap for working effectively with their boss. However, you can't simply throw the map on the person's desk and hope they can figure it out. You have to ensure the new employee can read the map. Create a process by which the person feels welcome, learns to read the map, and has an opportunity to ask questions about it so they join your team and organization smoothly and are able to be successful, efficient, and productive. Taylor's experience illustrates one way to go about this.

As a leader, being open and honest with yourself first and then with those who join your organization pays dividends. Set expectations up front as part of the onboarding process. Otherwise, you're setting yourself up for high turnover, and turnover in an organization is brutal. However, successful onboarding can lead to engaged productive employees and a thriving organization.

Expectations from the New Employee

It's also important to have new hires speak openly about their expectations—the earlier, the better. This ensures you're on the same page and enables you to understand what drives them. As part of any onboarding process, take time to ask new hires how they are motivated, how they work, what they expect from this role and their boss, along with how they like to be rewarded.

Often, individuals have never been asked what they expect; some have never even asked themselves either. If they know what motivates them, how they like to be rewarded, or how they like to hear bad news, it will be invaluable to you to know. If they don't know, the very fact of asking will get them thinking. In time, they will get clarity about themselves and provide you with a map to make your job easier and keep the turbulence to a minimum.

SLOW DOWN TO SPEED UP

Writing accurate, thoughtful, informative job descriptions takes time, as does crafting interview questions and creating a welcoming, consistent onboarding process. In your rapidly growing environment, you may be tempted to put a warm body in a chair or throw onboarding to the curb. Don't do it. If the data is correct, then the challenges caused by employee turnover can cost your company a lot of money—and create serious drag on timelines and processes. By spending time up front to hire and onboard well, you'll save yourself from this turbulence.

Even if you have all the right people in the right seats, challenges arise and communication slows. The next chapter discusses how you can increase retention and establish open communication channels so employees stay engaged, even in virtual environments.

TURBULENCE TOOLKIT

Assess

- How much does each new hire truly cost my organization?
- Have I worked on developing my own hiring expertise and HR skills?
- How often am I quick to hire and slow to fire, instead of the other way around?
- Does my organization create a new job description for each posting?
- Do my organization's job descriptions tell a story or merely list tasks and required credentials?
- Does the wording in my job description accurately reflect my culture and work environment?
- When was the last time I crafted a new question for an interview?
- Do I ask questions to discover attitude, coachability, and subtext?
- Do my interview panels represent diverse perspectives?
- Do we consistently onboard every employee?
- Is it time for us to revamp our onboarding process?
- When was the last time we asked a new employee to rate our onboarding?
- Do new hires agree they've been given clear expectations from the beginning?
- Do I ask new hires to articulate what they expect of us?
- Do I know what motivates my new hires and makes them feel rewarded?

Be Intentional

- Work to level up your hiring expertise, even if you have a hiring manager or head of HR.
- Slow down your hiring process so you don't have to go for the easy hire.

- Hire for where you are going, not just where you are.
- Clarify how culture will be communicated in postings and interviews.
- Create a Hiring Matrix to help you compare apples to apples and avoid gut feelings.
- Start posting in new and out-of-the-ordinary places to diversify your candidates.
- Co-create a deep and broad onboarding plan with your employees to ensure alignment of culture and expectations.
- Review and iterate your onboarding plan annually to address the changes that come with rapid growth.
- Articulate and clarify expectations on day one and ensure new hires are on the same page with their teams and higher-ups.

Pick One Thing

- Job descriptions
- Job postings
- Interview questions
- Hiring Matrix
- Onboarding

Dig Deeper

- *The Best Team Wins: Build Your Business through Predictive Hiring* by Adam Robinson
- *The Decision Book: Fifty Models for Strategic Thinking* by Mikael Krogerus and Roman Tschäppeler
- *Hire with Fire: The Relationship-Driven Interview and Hiring Method* by Denise Wilkerson and Randy Wilkerson
- *Hire with Your Head: Using POWER Hiring to Build Great Companies* by Lou Adler
- *Hiring for Attitude: A Revolutionary Approach to Recruiting and Selecting People with Both Tremendous Skills and Superb Attitude* by Mark Murphy
- SHRM.org

CHAPTER 6

TEAMS

THE POWER IN TEAM DYNAMICS

"If you want to know why your people are not performing well, step up to the mirror and take a peek."

—KEN BLANCHARD

Communication is like the circulatory system of a human body. It runs through every part of an organization. There isn't one employee, department, project, client, or decision that isn't touched by communication.

A clot in the human system doesn't just affect the body part where the clot occurs. It affects the dynamics of the whole organism, interrupting flow. The same is true of businesses. Leaders often overlook a challenge on one team or with one team member. They may think it will resolve itself, someone else will handle it, or it can be siloed within that group. This is never the case. Like a blood clot, a single miscommunication, misalignment, or unarticulated expectation in one area will be eventually felt company-wide. It may cause delays in projects, low morale, lost revenue, or a shifting culture that allows turbulence to not only persist but also intensify. If two co-founders are not getting along and fail to share vital information with each other, they will experience significant disruption, which will be visible to their team. If a team is working on a project that requires financial data and someone fails to secure it on time, the resulting proposal will either be late or wrong, impeding flow of the entire project. It takes only one clot to interrupt healthy dynamics.

As humans, we take our circulatory system for granted. Fortunately, the human body is a well-designed machine. However, we can't be that complacent with organizational communication. The work of maintaining effective communication is not sexy, but it is necessary for ensuring healthy team dynamics.

When a block in an organization's communication system occurs, leaders often attribute it to poor performance, bad hires, or ineffective managers. They may look for someone outside the organization who can find and fix the problem. However, the source of the obstruction is often found within the leaders themselves. A Gallup survey reported only 13 percent of US employees strongly agree that leadership communicates effectively with the rest of the organization.[23] That leaves a shocking percentage of leaders who may be missing a vital component for their business's success. If there is turbulence within a company, leaders must look in the mirror first to understand their own role in the stagnating team dynamics, engagement, and morale.

After they assess and own their part, leaders can build an intentional and well-defined process to improve communication flow and help the team work together productively. This begins with

---

23   "State of the American Workplace," Gallup 2017, https://www.gallup.com/workplace/238085/state-american-workplace-report-2017.aspx.

identifying and streamlining isolated cases of miscommunication as well as organization-wide turbulence. If a team isn't working well together, if retention is low, if employees are not inspired and engaged, then culture, timelines, financials, and more can suffer as a result. The results of ineffective communication need to be systematically addressed.

This chapter looks at the most common areas where ineffective or absent communication systems can cause turbulence—either between leadership and employees or within teams themselves. Disruptions can be mitigated or averted altogether by intentionally crafting and implementing a foundation of effective communication, both organization-wide and one-on-one.

THE LANGUAGE OF CULTURE

As discussed in our previous chapter, your company has a culture, whether or not you have intentionally crafted it. How your teams experience that culture comes down to what you communicate verbally and nonverbally. It's informed by what you do and what you don't do, along with how consistent you are with your message.

Your culture also has a language. It is seen in your organization's way of engaging and doing business. It shows up in who and how you promote. It shows up in how and when you fire people. It shows up in your company's social activities and staff meetings. Culture is a thread woven through every part of your organization.

After working with consultants and HR leaders to define the company culture, some organizations have a big kickoff and excitedly share a culture deck. However, crafting a strong, defined culture isn't enough. The language of your culture must be established, executed, and managed. That language ensures your culture reaches every corner of your organization.

Although defining the culture may be a one-time thing, the language of your culture must be embedded, monitored, and occasionally iterated or updated. When time isn't taken do this, the results can be measured in poor retention, slowed growth, and low engagement. All of these have the follow-on effect of negatively impacting everything from customer relationships to product delivery.

When you hear the term *company culture*, it is often associated with free lunches, social get-togethers, office layouts, and most recently, diversity and inclusion. All of these play a part in the culture. However, so does the frequency, tone, and outcomes of meetings; who gets promoted and how; and when and how people are rewarded.

DIVERSITY AND INCLUSION

Events in 2020 have finally led many companies to prioritize commitments to diverse and inclusive cultures. This is a positive and needed shift, albeit one that's been delayed for far too long. However, many companies run the risk of paying lip service to these values without doing the hard work of ensuring follow-through. A commitment stated must be a commitment fulfilled, or integrity and trust are lost.

I've worked with many companies that say diversity and inclusion are part of their culture. They usually have a web page dedicated to it with a statement such as, "We are committed to creating a workplace where everyone can feel valued and respected." If you ask leaders how that statement manifests and is measured across the organization, however, they couldn't tell you.

Consider your own workplace's culture of inclusivity. What is your organization's definition of *inclusive* and how is it measured? If you haven't taken time to define inclusivity, that's the place to start. That act alone will help you realize what you're doing and not doing to be inclusive.

How do you communicate to each employee that they are valued and respected? If each employee were to be interviewed anonymously, would all of them say they felt valued and respected? What do you reward or condone? Do you tend to reward those who have a big personality and readily showcase themselves over those who are nose-to-the-grindstone types? Either way is fine, but you have to be honest with yourself as an organization and with your employees so they know how to become successful in your company. The very act of asking these questions and assessing the answers gives insight into what you need to start or stop doing to create the culture you want to create.

I have known too many heads of DEI who have quit precisely because they were given a mandate to inform and transform the culture to be more diverse and inclusive, but they soon found the "commitment" and true culture did not support or align with the shift.

Worse than not being committed to a truly diverse and inclusive culture is issuing a press release or starting an ERG (employee resource group) but having a language of culture that clearly contradicts your stated commitment. ERGs are employee led, often unfunded or underfunded, and leadership rarely, if ever, shows up. This total lack of resources communicates to your team that the organization isn't truly committed to change. You can't simply say that you're committed to an ideal. Your commitment must be communicated in what you say, in what you don't say, in your actions, and in the actions you support and discourage in others. If you're going to have an ERG, for example, fund it properly and be an active participant. That's one place to start.

MERGERS AND ACQUISITIONS

A 2020 *Harvard Business Review* article puts the failure rate of mergers and acquisitions at 70–90 percent.[24] The reasons are many, but one particularly noteworthy factor is that merging companies often lack a common language of culture. Companies spend hundreds of thousands of dollars and hundreds of work hours aligning everything from the payroll system to the IT systems, yet no one bothers to assess the cultural compatibility or tries to align the different languages of culture. As a result, top talent—those who can easily find new opportunities—often leave within the first six months, creating company-wide disruption and potentially leaving the organization with unexpected and unwanted challenges.

Imagine a couple where one spouse is German and the other is Japanese. If they don't speak a common language, that marriage will likely struggle. The same is true when two companies merge. In a marriage of businesses, there must be a common language of culture.

---

24 Graham Kenny, "Don't Make This Common M&A Mistake," Harvard Business Review, March 16, 2020, https://hbr.org/2020/03/dont-make-this-common-ma-mistake.

TURBULENCE ALERT

A few years ago, I worked with an organization that had acquired a smaller competitor seven months prior. They found they were facing resistance from the employees of the acquired company resulting in significant turnover. The acquired company's clients were not happy either.

It did not take long to see how the diametrically opposite cultures played a major part in the turbulence they were experiencing. My client had a thriving business that was young and innovative. They had a culture of direct conversations, high expectations, and a demanding pace. The acquired company was smaller and long established. It had been run by the founder until they decided to sell and retire. The founder had not made many updates to processes or technology, and the organization had a culture focused on rewarding seniority, complete schedule flexibility, and even freshly baked cookies every Friday.

These cultures worked for each individual business. However, bringing the two together was like sitting down to a meal of caviar and Hot Pockets. They didn't belong on the same plate.

Given that the acquisition had already taken place, the goal now was to align the two cultures to provide a higher likelihood of long-term success. Aligning the cultures required finding a common language. It was a new language for both with elements and keywords from each. We looked at the language of hiring, onboarding, and rewarding. We reviewed social events and performance reviews. We found ways to align the definitions of success, urgency, and quality and how to engage effectively and consistently with all clients.

It took a focused commitment and continual work in some areas, but within two months of crafting a common language of culture, my client started to reengage employees from the acquired organization. Within six months, they won over the clients of the acquired company to the point that those clients were now making referrals.

With each merger or acquisition, the new organization will need time to understand, absorb, and finally embrace the language of the culture. It won't happen overnight, and it will require leaders to intentionally articulate where the old culture doesn't align with the new culture and then take steps to bring alignment. Finally, leaders will need to identify where and how they can consistently communicate that culture.

CLARITY AND CONSISTENCY

When you craft the language of your culture, you need to define terms. For example, what does *proactive* mean within your organization? What does *transparency* mean? You and I may define *transparency* very differently. I may think transparency in an organization includes knowing everyone's salary, but you may think it refers more to open, honest dialogue. It's not a matter of right or wrong; it's a matter of understanding what is meant in your organization when you use the term. Clarity matters.

In addition, you need to check in with team members across the organization to ensure what you mean is what they hear. Each organization can define their own metrics to measure the authenticity and alignment of their culture. This data is invaluable to ensuring and growing engagement throughout the organization.

One way to assess clarity and consistency around culture is to ask about it during exit interviews. Hearing different experiences can help you determine where there is unseen turbulence. You can also visit different offices and get a feel for the vibe in each location and assess whether it communicates the desired culture.

Different teams, departments, or offices may also have their own mini-cultures, informed by everything from their unique city, to workload, to leadership style. These mini-cultures can be essential to creating healthy team dynamics and engagement. However, they can't be so different that each mini-culture can't live under one organizational roof. The leaders at each level should verify that the organizational culture truly spans the whole company and that all mini-cultures align with it and are born out of it. If they don't, you end up with siloed teams, departments that don't want to work together, internal rebellions, and territorial fights, which cause turbulence at every level, even in the C-suite. The way to ensure that culture is consistent across the organization is through the shared language of culture: how the culture is articulated.

At the end of the day, the leader is architect and the keeper of the culture. It is their job to set, message, manage, assess, and iterate the language of their culture regularly. When a leader is absent or in any way unseen in this respect, there is little to no chance for consistency, growth, or engagement. Every level and layer of growth requires the leader to be present and not only update the language of their culture across the organization but also ensure it is threaded throughout the company. Language of culture binds your most valuable asset, your people, together. It increases the likelihood that everyone will be rowing in the same direction and avoid turbulence.

WALK THE FACTORY FLOOR

Culture and the language of culture relate to what you communicate to your teams. However, since communication is always a dialogue, it is equally important for you to hear the other side. One of the most reliable ways to do this is to literally or at least figuratively walk the factory floor. The term comes from old-school manufacturing plants where the machinery was on the ground floor and the executive offices were upstairs with windows overlooking the factory floor. The best leaders would periodically walk through the ground level to talk to people and find out how things were going.[25]

You might think you'll do this when you have five minutes to spare, but we all know how that works. It doesn't. To truly understand what is happening at all levels of your organization, you have to intentionally create a routine of walking the floor.

Physically walking the floor isn't always possible in today's world of remote and virtual offices and global organizations, but there is something powerful about walking around, overhearing conversations, asking questions, getting direct feedback, and engaging with people at all levels. Doing so puts you in their space, not them in yours, and opens the door to honest insights and feedback.

It is all too common, especially as an organization grows and becomes more and more successful, for a leader to be surrounded by people who may edit or not pass on information they do not see as valuable. Even worse is when the leader is surrounded by a yes-man sycophancy that keeps them from having an honest and full assessment of their organization. They

---

25   See Boris Groysberg and Michael Slind, "Leadership Is a Conversation," *Harvard Business Review*, June 2012, https://hbr.org/2012/06/leadership-is-a-conversation.

may receive monthly financials or updates on product development, but to truly know the pulse of their teams, leaders need to walk the factory floor, invite comments from all levels, and listen actively.

The reality TV show *Undercover Boss* is a bit contrived, but it illustrates well what happens when leaders walk the floor. In the show, CEOs of large organizations go undercover and work alongside the employees, loading pallets in the warehouse, cleaning bathrooms in the stadium, or preparing food in the kitchen. Inevitably, the CEOs go back to their hotel room at the end of the day and talk about how tired they are and how hard it was. They also share observations about what's not working—how employees are unaware of protocols or how broken equipment has gone unattended—and they note innovative and practical solutions only those on the front line can see.

If processes don't work or aren't being followed or if things are broken, it is essential that employees at every level be comfortable providing feedback. Their managers should then address the issues by passing the information up the food chain. If these steps aren't happening, though, it's not the fault of the people at the bottom. It is ultimately the leader's responsibility to know what is happening when they are not around.

At the same time, nobody knows better how to make things run smoothly on the front line than the people on the front line. Too often, decisions made in the C-suite are not practical or effective when implemented. To fix the problems, leaders should talk to those who will execute the new plan or work the new equipment, not someone three or four rungs up. Bring in the people who deliver that process on the front line and encourage them to contribute feedback, solutions, and upgrades. Have them co-create a new or improved process. In doing so, you will get buy-in and increase efficiency, both of which are invaluable for the organization as a whole.

Walking the factory floor makes you visible; it ensures your presence is felt and your interest is apparent. Granted, when there are multiple moving parts and you have commitments to a lot of people, it can be hard to find time to walk the floor. Later in this chapter, we'll discuss some potential virtual solutions that can help you check in with your people efficiently. Ultimately, however, the onus is on you to make it happen.

Engaging with your team is one of the key ways the language of culture is communicated. Ask questions, listen, walk into their space instead of requiring that they walk into yours—these are all ways to build a culture of engagement that values and respects your employees.

FLOW OF INFORMATION

How do you ensure that you are visible to everyone at every level of your organization? You may say that you want to hear from everyone, but there may be several organizational layers between you and the people on the factory floor.

I think of a growing organization as a multi-decker bus. When the business starts and operations are small, there is only one level. Everyone feels every bump and pothole on the road. As the company grows and the org chart expands, those at the top of the bus feel a smoother ride, while those on the first level feel every rattle and roll. The experience of turbulence is different depending on where you sit. As a leader, you need to sit in different seats to put yourself in others' shoes and understand the disruptions they feel.

Having multiple layers also hinders the free flow of communication both from top to bottom and, especially, from bottom to top. Sending ideas up to leadership often becomes a game of telephone, with messages completely changed by the time they reach your desk. Those in the middle decks may misinterpret feedback, overedit messages, or simply choose not to pass on all the relevant information. Messages from the top may change in tone and tenor as they travel down.

In reality, not every recommendation that comes from every one of your employees is something that can be implemented. Many factors go into leaders' decision making, and a suggestion that comes from an employee unfamiliar with those factors may not be feasible or timely. However, even if a suggestion won't work, it's powerful to make your employees feel heard. Thank them for the recommendation and explain why it won't work. If an element of their idea is something you'll hold on to for another time, let them know. This sort of affirmation creates engagement and promotes retention. It also makes people feel valued and respected.

LEADER AS COACH

When building an engaged, high-functioning, and productive team, a leader is most effective if they think of themself as a coach—the person who is developing individuals and the collective team. With time at a premium, leaders often focus on the sales, the timelines, or even the press. As a result, their most valuable asset—their people—are unattended or undersupported. Whether you act as an employee's direct coach or delegate to your assistant coaches, as the leader, the greatest success come when you develop your players and unify the team.

Ensuring a healthy, authentic, organizational culture that is well supported and consistent across the organization is a first step. Doing so creates a foundation for all of the teams. However, every good coach knows each team member requires a different approach because each one is unique. They vary in strengths and weaknesses, in confidence and coachability, in skills and qualities. Coaching is not about having them do it the way you would or you going on the field for them. It is about providing insights and the right tools so they can excel on the field. Developing a strong and healthy team requires effective and constructive conversations most commonly referred to as feedback.

Ken Blanchard famously stated, "Feedback is the breakfast of champions."[26] Unfortunately, research shows only 23 percent of employees strongly agree that they receive *meaningful* feedback.[27] As coaches, we must ensure our feedback is tailored to the needs of each player; otherwise, it won't be meaningful.

So what does meaningful feedback look like? Here are some suggestions.

START WITH THEM

As with many conversations, we often think about what we want to say when talking with our players when we should be focusing on what they need to hear. To know what they need to hear, we

---

26   Ken Blanchard, "Feedback Is the Breakfast of Champions," BK Blog, n.d., https://www.bkconnection.com/bkblog/ken-blanchard/feedback-is-the-breakfast-of-champions.

27   "State of the American Workplace," Gallup 2017, https://www.gallup.com/workplace/238085/state-american-workplace-report-2017.aspx.

must first get to know them. Identify each person's strengths, weaknesses, qualities, and potential, as well as their personalities and communication styles. Then you'll know how to coach each player effectively. This personalization will not only build up each individual but the team as a whole. Plus, if you understand each player, then when a certain challenge arises or productivity decreases, you likely already know where the turbulence is occurring and will be able to address it more quickly and effectively.

The DISC assessment mentioned in Chapter 1 can come in handy here. For example, some people need a direct, get-to-the-point assessment; these folks will likely leave the meeting with a bulleted to-do list. Others require a more conversational approach, talking through the challenges and outcomes. To process the feedback, they may not take notes, which means a follow-up email would help ensure they are clear on the themes and solutions. In each case, feedback should precisely fit the individual's communication style and include solutions or ways to lean into success.

ASSESSING VS. CRITICIZING

Conversations with your team are an opportunity for constructive feedback, but leaders often see these conversations as an exercise in negativity, a chance to list everything the employee needs to improve. That's not because there is nothing good to share. Usually, the absence of positive feedback is simply a by-product of being busy and making time for reviews only when something isn't going as it should. Even if leaders don't use negative terminology in the meeting, their tone and subtext may imply that the meeting is not a positive one. As soon as you start thinking of performance reviews and casual feedback as something negative, these conversations become easier and easier to push back or avoid altogether.

Leaders aren't the only ones who want to avoid these meetings. Let's be honest: employees aren't excited about them either. They worry that something isn't going well and come in braced for that news. The result is two people walking into a review anticipating that it will be an uncomfortable conversation. That's not a recipe for success. No one who feels they are being judged or criticized will walk away from a conversation inspired to make a change or motivated to work harder.

For feedback to be valuable, it should be free of judgment. Before a review conversation, ask yourself what you're planning to discuss and how the employee might respond to it. Will they perceive the feedback as negative, positive, or simply constructive? The answer will differ from employee to employee, as each has different drivers, personalities, and triggers. Even when you need to discuss areas for improvement, feedback is an opportunity to exchange data, knowledge, tools, expectations, and strategies delivered in a mutually constructive and nonjudgmental way.

If you only bring people in for reviews when something isn't going well or sweet talk them first to soften what follows, then you've trained them to anticipate negativity. Instead, make a habit out of celebrating small wins so that feedback is just as often delivered for positive reasons. It doesn't need to be formal. Some employees may appreciate a simple pat on the back and hearing, "Great job!" Others may be motivated by a staff meeting shout-out.

"FOR FEEDBACK TO BE VALUABLE, IT
SHOULD BE FREE OF JUDGMENT."

We tend to dive deep when someone doesn't get something right; doing the same with successes is powerful. Your team will find it valuable to understand not only that something has gone well but also what they did and how they achieved the success. Tools to replicate success are as important as the tools to improve misses.

TURBULENCE ALERT

In private conversations with me, Joe is complimentary about Matthew, a member of his team. Yet, whenever we meet in a group, Joe's real-time feedback to Matthew is always critical. There's never a celebration of the things he's done well.

As a result, Matthew has started saying things like, "Well, I can't do that because that's not how Joe likes it" or "That's not what Joe would want me to do." He's second-guessing every instinct because the feedback he's received is all related to the things he's done wrong. He has no data to provide balance and support of what is going well.

When I met one-on-one with Matthew, I said, "Joe has had you here for a number of years. You've been promoted. The evidence would prove he values you." Then I asked, "What qualities and skills do you bring to the team that you believe Joe highly values?"

The only thing Matthew could think of was loyalty.

When I asked Joe the same question, he gave me an impressive list of qualities he had never communicated to Matthew. Because Joe only shared the challenges, Matthew's confidence was shaken, which undermined the value Matthew brought to the team. That lack of confidence can create a domino effect of other challenges. And although not every employee would react this way, it is important to know that Matthew would.

Given the very nature of the words *hard* and *difficult*, it's human nature to walk into these kinds of conversations with a negative assessment. Maybe you don't understand why the employee didn't meet the expectation you set or why they chose not to use the tool you provided. These thoughts can lead to frustration and ultimately a judgmental mindset, which often appears when our employees think or work differently than us. To make our perspective more objective, it is essential that we step back and understand how those differences impact their behavior; what we see as a problem may only be a personality difference. By being aware of their motivators and drivers, we can learn how to communicate in a way they can hear.

We increase the likelihood of an effective conversation if the discussion involves simply putting up a mirror in front of the individual, reflecting the person's words and actions as they are, with no judgment attached. Providing a mirror like this starts with intention—that is, deciding ahead of the meeting that we are simply laying out facts, not declaring them good or bad. The other person may not like what they see in the mirror, but that's a separate issue. Our goal is to reflect, not project judgment onto what is there.

Think about the rearview and sideview mirrors on a car. They do not judge our abilities as drivers; they allow us to see our blind spots so we avoid accidents. We can do the same thing for our team members. By asking questions and performing 360 assessments, we can put up a mirror to actions, events, strategies, and skills in a way that creates self-awareness in the employee. Then we can co-create a plan that provides strategies and recommendations the person can put to use, not simply to improve what wasn't working but to continue to leverage something that was.

CADENCE

Over recent years, many articles have been written regarding the death of the annual performance review, and rightly so. If someone was struggling or succeeding in February, why wait until December to talk to them in depth about it? No parent would wait five days before providing guidance to a child. Why delay feedback for those who are at the heart of your organization's success?

Instead, employ a steady cadence of feedback—that is, a regular rhythm of touching base with employees about their performance. Rather than wait until the end of the year, seek to engage with someone in the moment to improve performance or reinforce success going forward.

With a regular cadence, these conversations will begin to provide the leader with a "user manual" for truly understanding and appreciating each employee. Ask what makes employees feel valued and heard. Learn how they like to hear bad news. Getting a sense of your employees' preferred communication style will streamline the conversations and allow you to more fluently speak their language.

Do you have a set schedule for providing feedback? Do you have weekly or monthly meetings, or do you give feedback as situations arise, whether positive or negative? A variety of plans can work, so long as they're consistent. Consistency is essential, as inconsistency itself offers a mixed message. You may not be giving feedback because the employee is doing a great job and you have nothing to say, but the employee may perceive it differently.

That consistency works best when applied across the organization. Creating a system or protocols for how feedback and team development are approached across the organization should be part of the game plan. Every assistant coach should be working from the same playbook.

The right cadence for your organization will be different than that of the organization across the street. There is no right formula. The key is to ensure it is frequent enough to provide the tools and support needed to develop and unify the team. Then ensure that the cadence doesn't fall by the wayside when rapid growth makes things hectic. It's okay to tweak the cadence from time to time. Simply communicate that change, and make sure the assistant coaches have the new playbook so that everyone can maintain consistency.

SCOUT YOUR ROSTER

As the team coach, you may also want to keep your eyes open for three types of players who can have a dramatic effect on the team as a whole: the Squeaky Wheel, the Tasmanian Devil, and the Diamond in the Rough.

The Squeaky Wheel may show up as the needy employee who isn't coachable. They're like the hypochondriac who constantly complains of ailments but doesn't take the prescribed medicine or follow the suggested exercise plan. No matter how much feedback or how many tools you give the Squeaky Wheel, nothing shifts. The challenge is that in trying to fix the Squeaky Wheel, you may end up spending excessive time and energy in vain. Worse yet, you may inadvertently communicate to others that it's okay to ignore feedback. Then you risk having an entire team of Squeaky Wheels.

For team members who are unable or unwilling to look into

the judgment-free mirror you've provided, the only option is to have an honest and direct conversation, not about the feedback itself but about their coachability or lack thereof. If they can learn to acknowledge their blind spots, coaching them to grow in other areas will become that much easier.

The Tasmanian Devil is a vortex of agitation, oppressive energy, and more often than not, negativity. They may dominate the team in tone or demeanor and rock the boat to such an extent that others go along to get along. Or they might simply leave everyone exhausted. There's some good news, though: the Tasmanian Devil may be coachable. In my experience, these employees are often unaware of how they show up and the effect they have on the team. You can support them by developing their executive presence with a focus on scaling back their energy and being present.

Whereas the Squeaky Wheel and the Tasmanian Devil can create disruption, disagreement, and disharmony in the team, the Diamond in the Rough may well be a solution for all three challenges.

In rapidly moving organizations, we often speed past people who do not make themselves seen and heard. Just because someone is leadership material doesn't mean they are always *seen* as leadership material. This is often the case with the Diamond in the Rough. Human nature is such that we'll first notice and often promote people who excel at tooting their own horn, but these people aren't necessarily the best for the roles, nor are they all leadership material. What is guaranteed is that there are amazing leaders who are not horn tooters. Making themselves seen and heard may be outside their comfort zone; it may not be a quality they've developed.

These Diamonds in the Rough may have a quiet, almost sub-terranean, productive influence on the team. They may be fully engaged and committed. Other players may go to these people for insight or support. These undiscovered gems may have strong institutional memory, making them invaluable in a rapidly growing organization.

Once you find the Diamonds in the Rough, developing them can happen in different ways depending on who they are and what needs to happen. Their manager might provide the needed support, or they might set up external training or meetings with an executive or leadership coach to help these players start lever-aging their untapped qualities and see themselves in a new way.

If leadership consistently looks outside to fill positions rather than developing Diamonds in the Rough, turbulence can result. Employees can feel like the company doesn't invest in them or there's no opportunity for growth, which causes challenges around morale and retention. By looking for Diamonds in the Rough within the organization, leaders give employees a reason to stay, which limits expensive turnover.

"JUST BECAUSE SOMEONE IS LEADERSHIP MATERIAL DOESN'T MEAN THEY ARE SEEN AS LEADERSHIP MATERIAL."

If you survey the troops, identify the Diamonds in the Rough, and then coach them, you will add much value to the organization. Over time, learning to keep an eye out for the undeveloped talent in your midst becomes a part of the culture, a practice you can instill in all your leaders. Encourage everyone to flag talent, high-light skills, and toot the horn of those who can't toot their own.

STREAMLINING STRATEGIES

I spoke in Chapter 1 about approaching feedback as a peer-to-peer conversation, speaking the same language, and using active listening. These tools increase the likelihood of productive and effective coaching conversations.

These conversational tools also allow leaders to co-create solutions. After we raise the mirror and the individual becomes aware of their blind spots, our job as coaches is to collaborate with them on next steps. This dialogue increases the likelihood of coachability and buy-in. A leader can provide strategies they themselves have adopted, or they may offer resources or suggest training. For example, some people are methodical thinkers who need time to digest information before they contribute ideas, so they often remain quiet in brainstorming meetings. They may see themselves as great listeners and not realize that by keeping quiet, others can perceive them as having nothing to contribute. This could be the factor preventing them from being recognized or promoted.

As part of my work with methodical thinkers like this, I often suggest they take improv classes to practice speaking up in the moment. Improvisation requires participants to not only be fully present, as discussed in Chapter 3, but also to contribute on the spot. That skillset can then be brought into a staff meeting, a brainstorm session, or a one-on-one conversation and streamline unseen turbulence that blind spot may have been causing.

No single leader can have all the best tools for each individual team member every time, since not every tool works for every person. In addition, a leader may determine they are not the best person to coach a particular player and look to someone in their network whose toolkit is a better fit. In their book *The Con-*

nector Manager, Sari Wilde and Jaime Roca highlight the value not only of connecting across the organization for development but also of building an environment of trusted peer-to-peer coaching. It's not only your assistant coaches who can provide support; the teams themselves can coach one another and provide new and potentially more effective strategies while building cohesion and a healthy dynamic.

ENGAGEMENT

Engagement is a buzz word often thrown around in business. Leaders often think of engagement as an indication of the health and strength of their team. This need to assess engagement usually leads to an annual or biannual survey, the results of which, good or bad, are discussed in a meeting and then often put in a drawer, never to be seen or discussed again.

However, talking about employee engagement, having a survey around it, even discussing the results of that survey do not result in engaged employees. You have to intentionally engage people. A recent Gallup poll showed that only 33 percent of US employees rate themselves as engaged. The same poll also showed that actively disengaged employees cost the United States $483–$605 billion in lost productivity annually.[28] Holy cow! We can't afford *not* to think of engagement as anything other than a strategic imperative. A lack of employee engagement results in the expected turbulence of low retention, low morale, and low productivity. Reversing all three is critical to the health of the organization.

Engagement is often thought of as a one-way street, something

---

28 "State of the American Workplace," Gallup 2017, https://www.gallup.com/workplace/238085/state-american-workplace-report-2017.aspx.

employees are required to do or feel toward the organization. In actuality, engagement is reciprocal. Think of a space shuttle docking at the space station: the shuttle moves closer and closer, and then at a certain point the mechanism on the space station itself connects with the shuttle. Engagement requires action by both parties. In the work environment, the tone, the message, and the process of engagement actually begins at the top.

Here is another time when a leader is a coach, communicating, developing, and supporting your players. Research shows that coaching can be indicative of increased employee engagement; 65 percent of employees from companies with strong coaching cultures rated themselves as highly engaged.[29]

"ENGAGEMENT IS THE BY-PRODUCT OF A STRONG CULTURE."

You can take several steps to encourage increased engagement; the individually focused conversations we've already discussed are a great place to start. A clear and compelling vision story allows your team to understand their why and where the organization is going, which will help them identify their work as meaningful. Precise and consistently articulated expectations ensure they know where they stand and how they are doing, which will help maintain positive morale. Trust in a credible and authentic leader can help them weather challenging times and maintain a commitment to their work. Finally, when leaders walk the factory floor and actively listen, employees will feel heard. They will be reassured that their work is integral to the organization's success.

29 "Building a Coaching Culture," The Human Capital Institute, October 1, 2014, https://www.hci.org/research/building-coaching-culture.

Engagement is not the goal. It is instead the by-product of a strong culture, effective conversations, and a leader who communicates across the organization with intention and purpose.

TURBULENCE ALERT

I was hired by a fast-growing consulting company that was experiencing multiple challenges due to several new hires, distributed teams, and understaffing. They had doubled the workload in just over a year, and the organization was starting to fray at the seams. Clients complained that communication alternated between spare and frantic. New team members were dropped into complicated engagements with little to no background or leadership. Communication channels were littered with long "reply all" emails, some of which were seen by clients. Senior and middle managers had backgrounds in consulting, but few had ever had to lead an internal team across projects.

This company wanted me to run two cohorts of my Leaders as Coach program. One cohort was with senior managers and the second with middle managers. We began with assessments and a process of clarifying expectations. As the weeks progressed, the participants started to understand how to better communicate their expectations and how their own communication styles might be helping or hindering these discussions. They began having conversations with their teams that went beyond tasks and deadlines. They also started helping their teams self-assess and clarify their own strengths and gaps.

Within a few months, their meetings, both internally and externally, became more constructive and efficient. Client satisfaction increased, and the feedback loop between leadership and employees netted valuable ideas. However, at the end of the contract, the CEO said that the greatest ROI of shifting the mindset from managing to coaching was the increased morale and engagement at all levels of the organization.

VIRTUAL TEAMS

Any actor will tell you that performing on stage and performing on film are different ways of working that require different skill-sets. The growing world of virtual teams is not dissimilar. Some industries have been working remotely for years. However, the realities of 2020 mean every leader now has experience running virtual, remote, or distributed teams.

An organization's ability to work virtually has many advantages; at the same time, however, whatever turbulence exists within the four walls of an office is often exacerbated when teams go virtual. When people are siloed, when they are literally out of sight working remotely, those challenges can grow exponentially.

The silos created by isolated, virtual work can make it easier to avoid addressing miscommunications. It's also easier for people to feel ignored and not heard, as if they're in a one-way conversation, and it's harder to engage with the team individually as well as collectively.

Whether your teams were always distributed around the country or the team is temporarily working from home, a clear plan for engagement and feedback with a regular cadence is more important than ever. The silence of working at home alone with infrequent direction, poorly articulated expectations, and few, if any, opportunities for spontaneous conversations can hinder teams from rowing in the same direction.

Engineering and product teams have long known the value of daily stand-ups or "scrums." For software teams, the stand-up is like the team's huddle. It is part of "agile development," a way of effectively and productively working through complex problems to ensure the team is functioning optimally. When you work virtually, the regular exchange of information, understanding of team dynamics, and even tone and nonverbal communication become exponentially more important. Without a focused and well-articulated communication strategy for how an organization engages virtually, new areas of turbulence can emerge.

The right strategy or communications process will depend on the organization, the team, and the leader. For example, the product development team at a large tech company might meet every morning for fifteen minutes to go through the current hurdles, whereas the leadership team at a boutique consultancy may have end-of-the-week wrap-ups.

Just as with face-to-face teams, the following areas can pose particular challenges for teams that are working virtually.

CULTURE

How do you communicate culture when there is no common environment? The key is to create a common experience. Supporting, communicating, and reinforcing culture when everyone is working remotely, in different offices, states, even countries is foundational for creating this common experience—especially for those working in a country where the culture itself plays a part in the work life.

Intentionally crafting a language of your culture that can be communicated and supported virtually is essential even if you think you don't need it. If 2020 taught us anything, it's that we can avoid turbulence by having a shit-hits-the-fan plan ready—a plan that focuses not on *what* to do but on *how* to handle and manage upheaval. Part of the plan should address how to communicate through upheaval and include everything from expectations about response times, to providing feedback, to onboarding.

TURBULENCE ALERT

My colleague Samantha started a new job three weeks after the pandemic shutdown. Even though finding a great opportunity in a trying time was exciting, integrating into a new organization, getting up to speed, and connecting with colleagues could have been challenging under those conditions.

In Samantha's case, however, the new company created a virtual onboarding experience as similar to their in-person experience as possible. On her first day, she received a welcome packet at her front door that contained the normal swag someone would receive on their first day, along with some extra goodies to support her work-from-home environment. These helped reinforce the organization's culture of support and personal attention.

Samantha's first day began with more than just filling out forms, setting up IT, and meeting with her new boss to clarify priorities and expectations. She also had a Zoom call with the group of people with whom she would be regularly working. They each provided valuable information like "If you need help with X, I'm the person to talk to. This is what my schedule looks like." People who couldn't be on the entire call at least got on to say hello and introduce themselves. It was like virtually walking her through the office. Samantha was not only introduced to the team; she was also given a roadmap for how the team works together and how best to communicate with them.

This went a long way to making her new job easier. She was given an introduction into what to expect at the company, how they work, and by extension, the culture.

One of the more challenging areas for communicating culture virtually is finding ways to connect socially and allow team members to meet and build common ground. When functioning in-person, most organizations have social events to help increase employee engagement: communal lunches, happy hours, weekend retreats, and so on. In a virtual setting, embrace the opportunity to find a way to create a similar experience with your teams. Work collaboratively to co-create and replicate a virtual experience that will reflect your culture. It is easy to let this slide when everyone has Zoom fatigue. However, finding even occasional ways to bring the connection and humanity back into work pays dividends.

The right choice of tools for the right tasks now becomes a part of the culture as well. Today's technology has provided organizations with a growing number of communications tools. Email, Slack, and Zoom, among others, have allowed organizations to have remote workers and distributed teams. The key is making sure you use the tech tool that reflects the culture and engagement style that you want for your company and ensuring it is consistent across the organization. I will not use Slack. I have enough to keep track of during my day, and Slack messages go unattended. Other organizations might only use Microsoft Teams due to security concerns with other apps. The key is ensuring you use the tech tool that reflects the culture and engagement style that you want for your company and that it is employed consistently across the organization.

However, it is important to remember that these are simply tools, like a pen is a tool. Using a pen doesn't make you a better writer. If your organization doesn't have a strong foundation for how to engage and communicate effectively, or if the language of your culture is unclear when in-person, these virtual tools do little good and will inevitably cause turbulence—unasked and unaddressed questions, collaboration that doesn't happen, duplication of efforts, decreased productivity, and more.

STREAMLINING STRATEGIES

Here are some ideas to make the virtual conversations more effective.

Give Others Time

With back-to-back Zoom meetings and phone calls, it can be challenging to find time to review documents, emails, and updates. Ensure you give others enough time to review the information before discussing it. To you, that may mean three hours. If the other person has a back-to-back schedule, they may need twenty-four hours. For me, there are few things more frustrating than getting materials to review fifteen minutes before a meeting. It can communicate either disorganization or a lack of respect for the other person's needs. You can create a shortcut for conversation by providing information with plenty of time.

Be Fully Present

One of the realities of virtual work is that we often jump from meeting to meeting in less than a minute, rather than the time it takes to walk or drive to a different office. As a result, switching gears and being fully present can be challenging. Add on Zoom fatigue and the energy required to remain present online, and the possibility of an unproductive conversation increases.

However, you can take steps to help yourself be more present. Reading the room isn't possible, but you can listen actively. Work toward that by actively limiting distractions. You can't do anything about the barking dog or sounds from your neighbor's remodel, but you can close your email. Turn off all tech notifications. Switch off the news in the background.

Making eye contact with the camera can also help minimize the temptations of any remaining distractions and give those on the other end the sense that you are connected. It may feel odd at first, but I find it helps me listen more actively.

Since being fully present can be exhausting, booking several short meetings will usually net better returns that one long one.

Finally, reach out each morning to ensure the person on the other end is ready, in the right mindset and able to be fully present. You have no idea what is happening offline, and they may not want to request a reschedule. By quickly touching base, you let them know the door is open if they need to make a change.

Respond

Be aware that out of sight can easily mean out of mind. Pushing back meetings or "jumping in" late can become routine when working virtually, and you can unintentionally ghost coworkers through delayed responses, all of which creates challenges for ensuring your team believes they are heard and valued.

Ghosting is also easier when working virtually. The solution is simple: don't do it. Although the content of an email or voice mail may not be a priority for you, it may be for the other person. I get that email inboxes and Slack threads can be endless, as are the demands on a leader's time, but it's still crucial to effectively engage with and lead your team. Your response can be as simple and quick as, "I received your email. Give me some time. I will reach out to you next Tuesday," or setting expectations ahead of time: "If you don't hear from me within three hours, ping me again" or "If you leave a message, I will always get back to you by nine the next morning." We often employ this practice with clients and customers; that's the whole point behind the "out of office" message. We should do the same internally.

In the absence of information, the human brain always goes to the worst-case scenario, so stop ghosting. The easiest way to avoid that turbulence is to send an interaction to let the other person know what's happening and what to expect.

Create a Communication Plan

It is not realistic for leaders to devote their time to random and continual interruptions in their workday. Not only is it unproductive; it isn't scalable. Creating a communication plan ensures not only that your team feels heard but also that you have the opportunity to hear from them—a way of virtually walking the factory floor. Think of it as you would any other automation tool: it may take time to set up this plan at the outset, but it will increase efficiency and outcomes in the end.

Get Creative

I have seen smart leaders find creative ways to provide their teams with structured opportunities to be heard. Some hold regular AMAs (Ask Me Anything) meetings. They stay until every question has been answered.

Some ensure employees can connect without disrupting workflow by having regular office hours. These allow the leader to block out the time in their schedule and ensure they can be fully present while providing team members with a forum for conversation. The length and frequency of the office hours depends on your organization, its size, and your commitments. Whatever time you set aside, consistent and productive office hours can net meaningful insights, increased engagement, and greater influence across the organization.

One clever client created an email address exclusively for employee feedback so these messages didn't get lost in his very full general inbox. He then sat down every Thursday morning and read through the messages. Each received a direct response or a forward to another team member. He also tracked them for common themes and recurring issues.

Building team cohesion can also be challenging. A creative colleague of mine took advantage of storytelling to create connection and understanding despite having over twenty offices across the country. She led casual interviews on video with employees across the organization from different cities, different departments, and different roles. The interviews were engaging, relaxed, and very well received. They allowed employees across the organization to get to know one another.

Finally, remember that there are people who, even in person, are less likely to speak up. That is compounded when virtual. To encourage dialogue, actively invite your employees to engage with you and provide feedback. This can make a big difference in keeping the lines of communication open, whether they are working from home across town or on another continent.

Virtual communication falls into one of two extremes: it's

either too structured and formal, which can make it hard to execute consistently, or it's too social and loose. Ensuring your organization's virtual communications strategy is aligned with your culture, uses the right tools, and is structured to provide productivity, dialogue, and successful outcomes can help your rapidly growing organization avoid various forms of turbulence.

SLOW DOWN TO SPEED UP

I love to watch rowers. There is nothing more beautiful than a scull slicing through the water. Working together, rowers move the vessel smoothly and effectively in silent unison. However, one person rowing in a different direction at a different pace or with a different style can tip the boat and lose the race.

The same is true of organizational teams, whether they are under the same roof or only connected via the internet. Any turbulence with one person or on one team can affect the whole group and impact productivity and morale. As a leader, you can strengthen your team dynamics by clearly communicating the language of your culture, having a free flow of information throughout the organization, developing your team through coaching conversations, and ensuring a virtual work environment that keeps people connected.

Whether in person or virtual, most teams experience one challenge on an almost daily basis: conflict. In the next chapter, we'll discuss a different way to look at conflict as well as ways to get realigned.

TURBULENCE TOOLKIT

Assess

- Does a cross section of my team describe my culture in the same way?
- Do my stated commitments align with the realities of the day-to-day culture?
- Do I have strategies or metrics to ensure my stated culture remains aligned?
- How often do I engage with employees I rarely see? Do I go to them?
- How many levels must communication travel from the factory floor to my office?
- When I provide feedback, do I share my answers or do I ask questions and allow the person to see blind spots without judgment? Do I follow-up with tools rather than directions?
- Do I actively look to co-create solutions with my team?
- Is there a practice across my organization to provide feedback with no judgment?
- Does my team receive equal amounts of positive versus negative feedback?
- Do we as an organization think of engagement as a goal or a by-product?
- Who in the organization is responsible for employee engagement?
- Do I have an organizational plan for communicating culture virtually?
- Do I actively encourage learning not just virtual tools but virtual communication strategies?

Be Intentional

- Spend the majority of your day coaching rather than doing.
- As the company grows, allow the stated culture to expand and iterate, not simply fall by the wayside.

- Check in regularly to ensure your culture supports your organization.
- Get out from behind the computer and go engage regularly across the organization.
- Ask and listen to employees who may find it hard to provide feedback.
- Ensure that the layers through which communication travels allow for accuracy.
- Build your own coaching skills and techniques.
- Use assessment tools such as the DISC, Myers-Briggs, and Hogan to help individuals look into their blind spots in a constructive way.
- Ask for as much feedback as you are willing to give.
- Think of the technology as simply a tool for communication, not the communication itself.

Pick One Thing

- Language of culture
- Diversity and inclusion
- Mergers and acquisitions
- Walk the factory floor
- Flow of information
- Leader as coach
- Engagement
- Virtual teams

Dig Deeper

- *Bring Your Human to Work: 10 Surefire Ways to Design a Workplace That Is Good for People, Great for Business, and Just Might Change the World* by Erica Keswin
- *Build It: The Rebel Playbook for World-Class Employee Engagement* by Glenn Elliott and Debra Corey
- *Can You Hear Me? How to Connect with People in a Virtual World* by Nick Morgan
- *The Coaching Mindset: 8 Ways to Think Like a Coach* by Chad Hall
- *The Connector Manager: Why Some Managers Build Exceptional Talent—and Others Don't* by Sari Wilde and Jaime Roca

- Culturati Summit: culturatisummit.com
- *Humanize: How People-centric Organizations Succeed in a Social World* by Jamie Notter and Maddie Grant
- *Leading and Engaging Remote Teams Workshops* by The Ariel Group
- *Let's Talk: Make Effective Feedback Your Superpower* by Therese Huston
- *The Non-obvious Guide to Employee Engagement (for Millennials, Boomers and Everyone Else)* by Maddie Grant and Jamie Notter
- *The Weekly Coaching Conversation* by Brian Souza
- *2019 Retention Report* by the Work Institute
- "42 Shocking Company Culture Statistics You Need to Know," BuiltIn.com

CHAPTER 7

CONFLICT

MASTER DISCOURSE WITHOUT DISCORD

"This [avoiding conflict] is one of the worst things we can do as leaders. It stifles debate, discussion, innovation, ideas, creativity, and so much more."

—MIKE ROBBIN

Conflict happens. Research has found that the majority of employees (85 percent) have to deal with conflict to some degree, and 29 percent do so "always" or "frequently."[30]

Differing opinions, perspectives, and styles can help with decision making and move growth and innovation forward. However, too often differences morph into something negative, something destructive, something turbulent—conflict.

At some point, the idea that we have to find a way to "get along" became the talking point for resolving conflict. I have never agreed with that. It's not realistic to believe we can get along with everyone

---

30 Workplace Conflict and How Businesses Can Harness It to Thrive, CPP, July, 2008, https://www.themyersbriggs.com/-/media/f39a8b7fb4fe4daface552d9f485c825.ashx.

with whom we work. We can, however, strive to communicate effectively and, in this way, avert, address, and resolve conflict.

Many people perceive conflict as two cars heading toward a head-on collision. It feels threatening and personal. In reality, conflict is like two cars in different lanes heading in two different directions. Rather than a head-on collision, conflict is a misalignment.

In redefining the word *conflict* like this, we take out the anxiety, discomfort, or even enmity associated with it. When we remove the discomfort or threat level, we can productively assess and address how to become realigned. Then, instead of viewing the conversation to resolve conflict as walking into a head-on collision, we can see it as figuring out how to drive in the same direction so we can achieve the desired outcome.

Most leaders agree that conflict is one of the biggest areas of turbulence in their organization. This is particularly true for growing organizations. With new products, new customers, new hires, strategic pivots, and the inherent uncertainties of business, the opportunity for misalignment is everywhere. However, if a leader takes the time to assess the source of the misalignment as a first step when faced with disagreements, the organization reaps the rewards.

ASSESS TO AVERT

For me, the image that best encapsulates misalignment is the "spaghetti bowl" of highways you often find at an interchange in big cities, where multiple roads crisscross. Everyone may say they are in the same place, but each is on a different level, moving in a different direction.

Assessing misalignment shouldn't be hard. It does, however, require us to step back and think through the reasons for the misalignment. This can be challenging if tempers, urgency, or personality clashes infuse a layer of negative energy, but understanding where and how we often become misaligned can help.

AREAS OF MISALIGNMENT

The following are some common areas of misalignment, especially in rapidly growing companies.

Goals

Goals, whether strategic or for an upcoming meeting, often go unarticulated, which opens the door to friction. Imagine two soccer players on the same team working toward different goals. That is not a winning formula.

The same is true in business. Goals for product development, new initiatives, or even a new hire need alignment to be successful. If co-founders in the early stages of a startup are not aligned in their strategic priorities or the direction for the company, major disruption will result, not just between the founders but within the organization as a whole. This misalignment may show up in investor meetings, staff meetings, and board meetings, and it can slow or even destabilize growth.

Values

The best leaders focus on creating a healthy culture as a strong component of their organization, and values play a big part in communicating that culture.

Many companies pay a consulting firm a lot of money to help them create their mission and values statement. They paint those values all over the walls and sprinkle them throughout the job descriptions and on their website. But the day-to-day reality is quite different from the words splashed around the building.

If leaders themselves don't live out the values and continually ensure the culture reflects them, employees will find themselves conflicted. The result shows up as low morale, mistrust of leadership, or low retention.

In Chapter 5, I emphasized the importance of culture in hiring. Ensuring new employees are aligned with your company values helps keep them engaged and motivated. I left a company because the reality of their values and culture did not match what they espoused, and I knew I would never become aligned. I wish I had known the truth up front.

Method

Another area of misalignment is method, which refers to an individual's way of working. With math, two people may complete the same problem using different methods and still arrive at the same answer. In business, using different methods sometimes leads to different conclusions, timelines, or decisions, and conflict inevitably ensues.

We all have different methods of addressing problems, making decisions, or communicating. For example, my preferred method of engaging with clients is in person. If that's not possible, then I prefer Zoom or a phone call, in that order. For me, texting is only for brief messages like "I'm running five minutes late."

However, other people prefer email or text over the phone. If I don't get aligned with my employees or clients on our correspondence method, the other person may ask a question via text that goes unseen for too long. Or my response by voice mail may go unheard. I always ask my clients their preferred method of communication at the beginning of an engagement to ensure we avert future challenges.

I find misalignment around method often shows up between leaders and their direct reports. The leader assigns a task or responsibility, but the direct report goes about it in a way that differs from how the leader would have approached it. This often leads to micromanagement or frustration. Getting aligned at the outset—having a conversation around your different approaches—can diffuse conflict before it even occurs.

Intention

Another common area of misalignment is intention. I use the term *intention*, but you might call it motivation or purpose. A meeting may have an "official" agenda, but we all walk in with our own internal agenda, or what we want to achieve. One person's intention may be, "I want to finalize the book cover today," while someone else may think "I want more time to work on the book cover." Whatever your internal agenda or intention, it will create conflict if you are not in alignment with the others in the meeting.

TURBULENCE ALERT

I worked with an organization that sent two individuals to a meeting with a prospective client. Ahead of that meeting, however, Cesar and Kelly did not discuss and align their intentions for the conversation. Cesar believed the purpose of the meeting was to get the client to sign a letter of agreement. Kelly, on the other hand, saw the purpose as getting to know the prospective client, more clearly understand their challenges, and then refine the pitch. As a result, Cesar and Kelly communicated two different messages. Cesar kept working toward the bottom line: asking for the sale. Kelly kept asking questions to gain greater clarity. The two became frustrated with each other, which became apparent to the prospect, and even worse, they failed to present a united front.

A potential client looking to spend thousands or tens of thousands of dollars a month with a company does not want to sense conflict in its representatives. The misaligned intention between Cesar and Kelly created unnecessary turbulence.

Information

Information is one of the two most common and potentially damaging areas of misalignment, but it's also the easiest to fix.

Information misalignment happens when people try to make a decision or take action based on different sets of facts. If one person is working from the latest report and another person didn't read this version with its significant changes, the likelihood that they will experience conflict is high.

Consider the current political environment as an example.

Gone are the days where everyone got their news from Walter Cronkite on CBS or John Chancellor on NBC. Today, siloed information channels mean people make different decisions and have different perspectives because they consume different information. Preexisting systemic differences are exacerbated by a deep misalignment of information.

The key to fixing information misalignment is to ensure that everyone involved in the decision making has the same set of facts—the same graph, report, dashboard, KPIs, and so on. By ensuring everyone is literally on the same page, information alignment is easy.

We all have different backgrounds, life experiences, and knowledge that influence how we assess the information we amass over time. With so many unique perspectives, it's no wonder misalignment occurs. When we articulate the experiences and perspectives that inform us, we bring people to our side of the table—or move around to their side—giving us the same starting point, which decreases the chances of direct conflict. It also allows for better decision making because everyone is looking at the problem from a more complete perspective. This is why diversity and inclusion are so important. We might still come to different conclusions, but at least we're starting from the same point.

Working virtually has opened the door to technological misalignment, which makes information misalignment more likely. Team members travel on different roads all day and inevitably move in different directions. Imagine that spaghetti bowl intersection of roads with cars all heading their own way (Figure 7.1). One road is email, one is Slack, one is Teams, and so on. The threads of conversation are long, winding, and often misaligned.

Chances are high that information traveling on one road will be missed by those traveling on another. This is why crafting a clearly articulated plan for virtual communication is so essential. Aligning your tech tools helps align the flow of information.

Figure 7.1. The information superhighways

Information is produced and consumed at a an increasingly rapid pace. Think about how much information crosses your desk, lands in your inbox, or gets discussed in meetings in the course of one day. Miss even one response in an email or Slack thread and *bam*—conflict. Information misalignment is so common that it often goes unnoticed or unaddressed, leading to continual underlying turbulence.

Expectations

Along with information, expectations are the most common area of misalignment, primarily because they happen so often. A growing organization has numerous expectations, from sales goals and deadlines, to job descriptions and daily tasks. Since clarifying and articulating expectations is not as common as it should be, misalignment happens.

Conflict resulting from misaligned expectations usually happens for one of two reasons: (1) you didn't set clear expectations, but you are still holding someone to them, or (2) you expressed expectations, but each person understands and/or interprets them differently. If your expectations differ from what the other person thinks you expect, there will be conflict. Someone will fall short of meeting expectations.

The biggest tragedy I see around misalignment of expectations is people who get fired but feel blindsided. This happens when the leader believes they set and articulated expectations and followed up with feedback, but the employee believes they met expectations when they have actually fallen short. In such cases, the leader likely has not taken the time to ensure the employee is on the same page.

Remember, it is not your team's job to understand you; it is your job to be understood. If someone does not understand what you're saying, repeating it over and over is like going to a foreign country and saying something slowly and loudly in English. The other person won't understand unless you restate your expectation in their language.

Clearly articulated, precise expectations give the employee the tools to be successful. Providing clear feedback on where and why expectations are being met, or not, increases the likelihood of alignment, averting conflict and increasing productivity and growth.

Consider expectations related to a deadline. A leader may communicate that they need a report ASAP, but that is not precise. What is the leader's definition of ASAP? How does the individual tasked with providing the report define "as soon as possible"?

If the employee's calendar is booked with priority work for the next two days, they may not return the report until the third day. From the leader's point of view, the expectation was not met. In the employee's mind, they did the work ASAP. If the leader had simply stated that ASAP meant noon on Tuesday, or if they had asked how quickly the employee could finish the report, the two would have aligned and conflict could have been averted.

ASSESS THROUGH DIALOGUE

Alignment doesn't mean you agree on every point. It simply means that you're articulating and working from the same foundation. The reality is that once you are all on the same page—whether it's goals, expectations, or information—there may still be disagreement. If it still feels like conflict, however, you have a bigger challenge: Are these the right people on the team? Is this the right decision for the organization? If the board and leadership can never align on a goal, that's a bigger problem and the answer to fixing it will be different for every organization. What matters in the end is having the honest conversations.

In addition to those discussed here, there may be other areas of misalignment, such as priorities and definitions. At the end of the day, the process to become aligned on any of these areas is the same: conversation. Ensure you understand what lane the other person is in and in what direction they are headed. Let them know your point of view, share your sources of information, clarify your expectations, or articulate your goals and intentions. It goes back to Chapter 1: have the conversation.

Assessing where you are experiencing misalignment is the first conversation; the second is addressing how to become realigned.

ADDRESS THE CONFLICT

Sometimes conflict cannot be averted, and then we have to address it. The goal is to mitigate the effects of the misalignment and how much turbulence it creates, and two tools can help to this end. If you don't leverage these tools, you are likely to make the situation worse.

COMMUNICATION STYLES

The CPP report *Workplace Conflict and How Businesses Can Harness It to Thrive* found that the number one reason for conflict is seen as personality clashes and warring egos. This is because how we address conflict can compound the conflict itself. Addressing the conflict involves how we engage with people when we feel like we are in conflict.

When we are frustrated or feeling at odds with someone, we often avoid eye contact or choose words that are more divisive or tinged with judgment. This only adds another layer to the conflict. Even simply worrying about conflict affects our tone, energy, and body language, which communicates so much before we ever open our mouths to address the challenge. (As discussed in Chapter 3, a person's presence can impact conflict in either a positive or negative way.)

TURBULENCE ALERT

Marcus is a CEO who has had repeated conflict with a certain board member. From Marcus's perspective, they simply didn't see eye to eye. Going into one board meeting, Marcus was in direct conflict with this person about a strategic initiative and the changes needed to achieve it. He walked into this meeting knowing it would be contentious. During the meeting itself, he avoided eye contact with that board member and didn't address him directly in conversation.

As a result, the board member felt that Marcus was avoiding him, dismissing his point of view as unimportant, and might even be scared to look him in the eye. This exacerbated the conflict. Originally, they were simply misaligned about what decision they should make for the business, but Marcus's negative presence intensified the tension. This not only created turbulence in the meeting, but it also undermined Marcus's credibility.

Whatever our authentic executive presence, it always intensifies when we are stressed, under pressure, or frustrated. If we understand this ahead of time, then we can slow down and set an intention for how we show up when we address conflict. Understanding our communication style under pressure is a powerful tool that can help us streamline turbulence before we plunge right into the thick of it. Slowing down like this may take more time, but it is certainly easier than cleaning up the mess we can leave behind if we don't.

STREAMLINING STRATEGY

To help clients better understand their communication style and how they may be perceived when addressing conflict, I like to use the Thomas-Kilmann Conflict Mode Assessment. It outlines five conflict-handling modes, or styles: competing, accommodating, avoiding, collaborating, and compromising. The assessment places the five styles along two axes: assertiveness (energy, tone) and cooperativeness (active listening and conversations). We all have a natural or default style, but it may not be the right one for each situation. Whatever your default mode, you can learn to dial it up or down, based on the situation, environment, and individuals in conflict.

In providing an organization-wide strategy for how you and your teams address conflict, the Thomas-Kilmann Conflict Mode assessment and a DISC assessment are invaluable. If everyone is aware and speaking the same language, alignment becomes easier.

AVOID AVOIDANCE

The second tool for addressing conflict is avoiding avoidance.

When presented with conflict, it is human nature to want to avoid it. That swerve to avoid the head-on collision is instinctive. We do it without thinking; it feels connected to our survival. That same instinct to swerve can be found at the office. However, avoiding a conversation, meeting, or individual is guaranteed to make any conflict worse.

Research has even put a number on the cost of conflict. Based on an average hourly earnings of $17.95, the study reports that $359 billion in paid hours (the equivalent of 385 million working days) is wasted each year in the United States because of conflict.[31] This number is so high in large part because conflict is often avoided, which draws it out and exacerbates the issues.

---

31   CPP, Workplace Conflict and How Businesses Can Harness It to Thrive.

So why do we avoid conflict? Avoidance is easy. Addressing the conflict feels unnatural. If we see the situation as conflict, we assume addressing it won't go well or go the way we want. We worry that it will make us look bad or that someone may feel hurt. In fact, we'll look for a million reasons to avoid it. "I don't have time." "I'll do it next week." "John will handle it." The list goes on. We might not even define what we're doing as avoidance. We might think we are delegating or procrastinating.

At the same time, simply having the conversation is not enough. Sometimes avoidance shows up as the "compliment sandwich"—you know, that meaty truth between two slices of bologna. Framing a conversation around misalignment in this way allows the listener to hear what they want to hear. If the first and last statements are positive, they often miss or dismiss the meat in the middle, either because they forget it or assume it isn't important. Being direct does not equal being aggressive or mean. Aggression is about tone and energy. Directness is about getting to the facts, which helps the listener remain focused on the message instead of the fluff. Having the conversation without being direct and transparent is still avoidance and will still create unnecessary turbulence.

Too often, I have found that a key player on a leadership team in conflict has taken on the role of Chief Avoidance Officer, the person who is constantly avoiding uncomfortable situations and conversations. Hopefully, this isn't you. If you regularly avoid certain conversations, you could be hurting your career as well as your company.

TURBULENCE ALERT

One of my clients had an employee, Tim, who had to let someone go. Tim was so stressed that he kept avoiding the conversation he needed to have with Dave. Ultimately, it created an issue well beyond his department. Tim ended up in conflict with his boss (my client) because he would not have the conversation.

Tim avoided the discussion for what seem like plausible reasons. First, Dave was Tim's first cousin. (That makes for awkward holiday dinners.) Also, Tim and Dave started at the company at almost the same time. Tim had moved up, but in its rapid growth, the company had outgrown Dave's abilities. Still, even though Tim's reluctance to address the issue was understandable, avoiding it was unacceptable. The organization was relying on Tim to do his job, however hard.

Tim could have taken several actions to avert or at least mitigate the conflict. By avoiding it, however, Tim not only failed to resolve the issue Dave's job performance had created, but he also undermined his own credibility and authority with his boss.

My client ended up having to fire Dave. He was no less inclined than Tim to avoid the situation, especially since Dave was not his direct report. The idea of telling someone they no longer have a job is uncomfortable, and my client was concerned the meeting would be confrontational.

Since it would not be helpful to walk into the meeting believing there would be conflict, we addressed the conversations my client was having with himself. He created an intention of letting Dave do most of the talking while he used active listening to determine how to find alignment and have the conversation he needed to have.

My client started the dialogue with "I wanted to check in with you about how you're feeling about your role and what's been going on. Do you feel you're in the right role? Are you feeling like you are able to leverage your skills?" Dave ultimately admitted that he was not happy, that he was in the wrong place, and that he wanted to change because he knew he was letting people down. More importantly, this situation had caused Dave to hate his job. No one who hates their job is going to be good at it, no matter what their skills.

At that point, my client didn't have to do much else. The conversation was honest, respectful, and nonconfrontational. The next day, Dave actually sent my client an email saying thank you. Who says "thank you" when they get fired?

Because Tim had avoided the situation for so long, he had created turbulence that caused bigger and bigger problems across the organization. If he had taken the time to have a conversation with Dave, so much disruption could have been avoided.

SLOW DOWN TO SPEED UP

Conflict on teams, with a board, or among leadership executives is one of the main reasons clients reach out to me. In the world of turbulence, conflict is the most evident, the most destructive, and the biggest drag on growth. There is no one right answer for resolving conflict that works for every department, every team, every organization. There's no magic formula. If I had the magic fairy dust to solve every conflict in every situation, I would be selling that instead of writing this book.

However, there is a consistently positive place to start with addressing conflict: learn to see conflict as misalignment instead of a head-on collision. In doing so, the conversations you need to have will feel less threatening and you'll be more likely to have them. And the more you slow down and assess why you might be misaligned, the chances of overcoming that sense of conflict and resolving the situation will go up exponentially.

In the last chapter, we'll look at how you can leverage your It Factor as the foundation of your leadership.

TURBULENCE TOOLKIT

Assess

- Can I quantify the number of hours per week my employees spend managing conflict?
- Does my organization articulate a process or approach to conflict as part of our culture?
- Do I think of challenging conversations as head-on collisions?
- What is the most common form of misalignment in our organization?
- Do work-from-home silos and/or technology create information misalignment?
- When was the last time I ensured my leadership team was aligned on vision, values, and goals?
- Do I regularly check in with how expectations are articulated to ensure averting conflict?
- Do I know my default conflict style?
- Do I know how my authentic presence shows up when in conflict?
- Have I avoided a conversation or an individual in the past week/month?
- Do I use delegation as a form of avoidance?
- Does my organization have a Chief Avoidance Officer?

Be Intentional

- Endeavor to keep the idea of a head-on collision at bay.
- Check in with yourself to figure out how you are approaching the conversation, situation, or person.
- Stop and assess where you may be misaligned.
- Craft a practice of assessing misalignment through dialogue across the organization.
- Have conversations to assess misalignment rather than the topic of conflict.
- Avoid avoidance.
- Assess your conflict style and when it serves or undermines you.

Pick One Thing

- Reframing conflict
- Areas of misalignment
- Conflict management style
- Executive presence in conflict
- Avoidance

Dig Deeper

- *Difficult Conversations: How to Discuss What Matters Most* by Douglas Stone, Bruce Patton, and Sheila Heen
- *Listening to Conflict: Finding Constructive Solutions to Workplace Disputes* by Erik J. Van Slyke
- *Optimal Outcomes: Free Yourself from Conflict at Work and Home* by Jennifer Goldman-Wetzler, PhD
- Thomas-Kilmann Conflict Mode Instrument (TKI®): KilmannDiagnostics.com
- *Upstream: The Quest to Solve Problems before They Happen* by Dan Heath
- *Why Great Leaders Don't Take Yes for an Answer: Managing for Conflict and Consensus* by Michael A. Roberto

CHAPTER 8

AUTHENTICITY

USE YOUR IT FACTOR

"Authenticity is a collection of choices that we have to make every day. It's about the choice to show up and be real. The choice to be honest. The choice to let our true selves be seen."

—BRENÉ BROWN

Being authentic should be the easiest thing we do every day. After all, it's just a matter of being our genuine selves when we walk into the office or engage with others. However, article after article these days is written about authentic leadership. Why is there so much discussion about something that should come naturally?

The truth is, as we go through life—our work life in particular—we pick up habits. We consciously and subconsciously observe those in leadership. We watch interviews with power players. We identify role models. We look to magazine covers and conference keynote speakers for the style and path to success. Out of a feeling that we need to look the part, we occasionally take on qualities we admire or think are necessary to be successful.

Sometimes, however, these traits don't fit us. It's like stepping into someone else's suit. It might be beautiful, but if it doesn't fit, we'll feel uncomfortable and others will notice something is not quite right. Just as no two actors play Hamlet the same way, no two genuinely effective leaders have the same unique style or leverage it the same way. If we try to be someone we're not, we come across as inauthentic or, worse, untrustworthy.

Research shows that leader authenticity can have powerful outcomes for organizations. One study found that "employees who perceived their entrepreneur/leader to be more authentic had correspondingly higher levels of organizational commitment, job satisfaction, and work happiness."[32] When commitment, job satisfaction, and work happiness are high, productivity and financial outcomes also improve, so there is good reason to pursue authentic leadership.

When working with clients, I define authenticity in two ways. The first is "not copied." I find this helps frame an individual's authentic leadership style as unique and original to them rather than like anyone else. The second is "true to oneself." This becomes an internal measuring stick to keep us authentic when work becomes hectic and turbulent. Essentially, your authentic leadership style is your own distinct and powerful language, which you can leverage to build credibility and influence.

There are also two chief misconceptions about authenticity. The first is that being authentic is somehow related to being liked; the second is that there can only be one genuine you, rather than being a multifaceted individual. In this chapter, we'll discuss

---

32   Susan M. Jensen and Fred Luthans, "Entrepreneurs as Authentic Leaders: Impact on Employees' Attitudes," Leadership and Organization Development Journal 27, no. 8 (2006): 646–666.

these misconceptions as well as how you can avoid turbulence by leveraging and leading with your It Factor.

AUTHENTICITY VS. LIKABILITY

Authenticity is not the same as likability, yet for some reason the two concepts have become conflated. People think that being authentic means people will know you and, by extension, like you. There are plenty of fully authentic assholes who have found a way to lead successfully and effectively. Those who worked with Steve Jobs described him as autocratic, demanding, and abusive in his interpersonal conduct, wholly unlikable in many respects. But as his biographer Walter Isaacson stated, "The essence of Jobs, I think, is that his personality was integral to his way of doing business." Guy Kawasaki, who worked at Apple for years, said, "It wasn't easy to work for him; it was sometimes unpleasant and always scary, but it drove many of us to do the finest work of our careers."[33]

I am not suggesting that you be "scary," "autocratic," or an asshole. Frankly, this style would likely only work well for Steve Jobs. I am suggesting that you put aside the idea that you must be likable and focus on leading with *your* authentic self. This is the foundation to leading effectively.

Likability is not a constructive goal. We cannot control whether people like us; that's based on their perceptions. It's sometimes challenging, especially for first-time leaders, to move from team member to team leader. Both sides feel the shift, and those new

33   Walter Isaacson, "The Real Leadership Lessons of Steve Jobs," Harvard Business Review, April 2012, https://hbr.org/2012/04/the-real-leadership-lessons-of-steve-jobs; Guy Kawasaki, "At Apple 'You Had to Prove Yourself Every Day, or Steve Jobs Got Rid of You," Make It, March 1, 2019, https://www.cnbc.com/2019/03/01/former-apple-employee-guy-kawasaki-once-stood-up-to-steve-jobs-here-is-the-amazing-response-he-received.html.

leaders often find it difficult to accept that they may be disliked or out of sync with their teams. That's human. Let's face it, being disliked sucks for most of us. Leaders want others to follow them, and likability seems essential to this outcome.

However, being liked isn't what matters. It doesn't ensure people will follow you. Being *trusted* is what matters. A trusted leader is a great leader. Being inspiring, dynamic, confident, trusted—those qualities are at the core of leadership and make others willing to follow you.

The challenge here is to understand your own leadership style, embrace it, and lead with it. You have to be okay with the fact that some people may not like your style. They may not understand you. They may find you too direct or soft spoken. However, if you are authentically yourself and lead with your own style, your confidence will inspire people to trust you. They will know what to expect of you. If people trust you—if they believe you and if you lead them well—then being liked will be irrelevant.

The conflation of authenticity and likability happens often, and it distracts us from showing up with our teams, our clients, and our investors in a way that is sustainable and productive. I've known leaders who were not just liked but beloved by their teams, but in several cases, organizational growth was slowed or stifled because a focus on likability made difficult conversations easier to avoid and changes harder to implement. As a result, decisiveness became tainted with thoughts about how it would be received rather than what was best for the organization.

Remember, you don't have to get along with everyone you work with, but you do have to communicate effectively with them. Effective communication becomes easier as we own our authentic style and bring it to work every day.

THE DIMENSIONS OF AUTHENTICITY

We are not one dimensional, either as people or as leaders. We have varied interests and qualities. When we are stressed, we show up differently than we do when we are having fun with friends. I may show up with different energy or intention with startup founders than I would with the managing director of a large established firm. Showing up in these various ways does not mean I am being inauthentic in either case. These are simply different aspects of who I am.

We are all diamonds with many facets. Being authentic doesn't mean we have to show all of our facets, all the time, to every person. It also doesn't mean we show up in exactly the same way in every situation. Although we all have certain default settings—energy levels, qualities, personality traits—we also have the ability to dial those settings up and down depending on the scenario. Doing so isn't inauthentic; it means we can read the room and show up in an authentic way that supports our intention and leadership goals without bending ourselves backward to fit in.

The same is true of our natural leadership style. Although we all have a way of leading that is ingrained in everything we do, we can dial it up or down, like a stereo. I have worked with several large, prestigious law firms. Anyone who has walked into an office like theirs knows the atmosphere is refined, hushed, and often intentionally intimidating. *Hushed*, however, is not an attribute of my authentic leadership style. Frankly, my style is the opposite of "hushed." My work requires me to be highly verbal—in meetings, brainstorming, and public speaking. I was also raised in a family of loud Spaniards, so even my "inside voice" and energy are a bit higher than most.

I am not a supporter of the "fake it till you make it" school of thought. So when I need to lead a meeting with one of these big law firm clients, I don't fake hushed, primarily because that would be inauthentic. It would also require too much energy to maintain speaking in a softer tone and keep my body language reined in. If I were to lose focus for one minute, my facade would likely drop. Instead, I begin with an awareness of their culture and atmosphere. I also let them know my style, which usually buys me some goodwill. Then I turn my dial down from my default seven to, say, a one. My one may still be higher than their default, but it's authentic to me.

Negating who we are to fit in is exhausting and, in the long run, not sustainable. I may be a bit more animated than the attorneys at these firms, but that energy works for me and, by extension, for my coaching. Inauthenticity doesn't threaten to undermine trust and connection with my clients. Meryl Streep said, "Acting is not about being someone different. It's finding the similarity in what is apparently different, then finding myself in there." That's authentic leadership. Once we are comfortable and at ease being ourselves in every situation, credibility, influence, and trust follow.

CONSISTENCY

Leading with different facets, dimensions, or positions on the dial is not the same as showing up in a way that's inconsistent with who we are. Dialing down my volume or energy is one thing, but if I were to show up as the soft-spoken, go-along-to-get-along type, that would be inauthentic and inconsistent with who I am.

Inconsistency kills credibility. This is especially true in relationship to our leadership style. If one individual knows you one way and a second knows you a different way, you risk losing the trust and respect of both. If they have very different versions of who you are, what happens when they compare notes? Your inconsistency will undermine your message and credibility.

Companies create protocols and processes to ensure their clients have consistent experiences. Imagine two friends go to a spa. They go off into separate rooms to get their massage. As part of the experience, one friend also receives a foot and scalp massage while the other does not. The therapists' inconsistency in their protocol would compromise the spa's brand and business. Imagine the conversation between the two friends afterward and the scathing Yelp review from the one who didn't get the extra treatments. In the same way, if every employee, client, or board member has a different experience engaging with you, they're not going to come away with a positive impression of your leadership.

TURBULENCE ALERT

I once worked with an executive who exemplified inconsistency in the way she showed up with different people. I was one of her senior leaders. During one of our weekly meetings, she received a call, and from the caller ID she saw that it was a member of our board. She took the call, but said I could stay.

When she answered the phone, her voice dropped about two octaves. She continued the entire conversation in that artificial, lowered voice and deferential tone, without the engaging style I was used to seeing from her. When she hung up, she returned to her "other" self for the rest of our meeting.

What kind of facade or mask was she putting on for that board member, that she didn't put on with me, a member of her senior leadership team? This situation made me see her in a new light. Her artifice made her seem tentative and unsure on the phone. The board member may not have noticed, but I did.

My perception of her changed that day. This happened over fifteen years ago, but the glaring example of inconsistency and inauthenticity has stuck with me.

It's hard enough to get through the workday when you are 100 percent authentically you, but showing up as someone else requires a tremendous amount of energy. It's the difference between going through your day in a pair of newly washed, skin-tight jeans or in a pair of yoga pants. The latter allows your body to be whoever you are at that moment. The former simply makes you aware of how uncomfortable you are.

ADMIRE, DON'T EMULATE

From a young age, we learn about leadership from those around us, perhaps a parent, a coach, or a teacher. Researchers have come to see mirror neurons as the biological mechanism through which humans unconsciously copy the behaviors of others. Every boss we have along the way informs our understanding of leadership, and role models are important, even essential. However, that doesn't mean what we learn or absorb is always good, or that those leadership styles are authentic and effective for us.

I admire people who lead with reserve, who are deliberate in conversations and in their decision making. But admiration doesn't mean I can lead with reserve. My style is more off-the-cuff. This doesn't mean I don't listen or take information into account. In fact, I produce much better work if I engage and process in the moment and offer insights on the spot than if I go off to sift through ideas on my own.

When we see someone we admire, it's easy to think we need to copy them to achieve their level of influence. That is a recipe for disaster. Some industries seem to crank out clones of professionals who use the same jargon, wear the same uniform, and make the same moves. After years working in the film business, I am well acquainted with such clones; some might call them posers. These people may talk the talk, but they rarely, if ever, inspire others to follow them. Think of it this way: do cover bands ever have the following of the original?

Don't turn yourself into a pretzel every day when you leave the house, trying to be someone you think you should be at work or behaving in a way you think matches what success looks like or what others expect of you. That is not a long-term plan for success. That is not leadership. That's follower-ship and that's imitation.

In her book *Mirror Thinking: How Role Models Make Us Human*, Fiona Murden says that when seeking out role models, you should start with a general sense of what you might need to fulfill your potential and then choose a role model accordingly. Instead of emulating these people or copying their behaviors, identify the *traits* you admire and find ways to integrate them in your own way. In doing so, you'll still have a chance to benefit from these mentors but won't sacrifice your own authentic leadership along the way.

AUTHENTIC LEADERSHIP

Leading authentically requires that you embrace who *you* are, what *you* lead with—your It Factor. Some people lead with humor, others with charm, still others with positivity. There are almost as many styles as there are leaders, and one way isn't better than another. The key is to learn what you lead with, embrace it, and lean into it.

Think of some high-profile leaders in modern history. We can go back to Steve Jobs. He led with ideas. Angela Merkel, on the other hand, leads with a quiet, stoic confidence. Both were or are successful in their sphere of influence, but they did not lead in the same way.

Here are a few examples of past and present high-profile leaders who have led authentically and consistently in their default leadership style:

LEADER	LEADS (OR LED) WITH
Martin Luther King Jr.	Gravitas
Elon Musk	Outlandish vision
Nelson Mandela	Compassion
Pope Francis	Humility
Teddy Roosevelt	(Bullish) vigor
Malala Yousafzai	Courage
Stephen Hawking	Intelligence
Fred Rogers	Empathy

As pointed out earlier, you are not one dimensional. You are a compilation of many traits and attributes. However, as you lean into your authentic strengths, it's likely that one will come to define your leadership. That is your It Factor. It's the thing people most associate with you and the reason they follow you. It is not the *whole* of your authentic leadership; it is simply a defining factor of *how* you lead.

Winston Churchill possessed wit and purpose, but the main reason people followed him was his grit. He walked the streets after bombings. He held firm when others were giving up. There were plenty of people, even some in his own party, who did not like him or agree with him. In the end, however, they did follow him. Owning your It Factor commands respect and leads to great leadership.

STREAMLINING STRATEGY

Deep down, most people know what their It Factor is, but they may not have articulated it to themselves. Alternately, they may not think of their It Factor as compelling, so they don't *lead* with it.

When I help my clients identify their authentic leadership style, I ask them to remember that it is an exercise in self-assessment—not self-criticism. When coaching your teams, you provide them with a mirror to see themselves without judgment; similarly, you have the opportunity to put a mirror up to yourself to define and refine that unique It Factor that will take you even further as a leader.

First, ask yourself, "How would others describe me when I am at ease and feeling comfortable in my own skin? What's the first attribute they notice?" It is not that you don't embody a long list of other attributes, but what do people see *first*? What's at the front of the parade? We may leverage different facets at different times, but there is always one main thread that characterizes who we are. We all have a default setting, our It Factor.

Second, talk to people who currently work for you or have in the past—not those who are senior to you or who are your peers but rather those you are leading or have led. Ask these people why they follow or followed you—not why they worked for you or did their job, but why they followed you. That may sound like an odd conversation to have with someone. However, everyone I know who has been bold enough to have it has walked away with insights to their authentic leadership style gleaned from a powerful and meaningful conversation.

With my clients, the discussion around why people follow them is very organic. There's no structure. I don't give them a document to fill out. I might ask, "What makes you good at this work? Not what tasks can you do, but what *quality* do you have that makes people want to follow you? What do you bring to the table that makes you trustworthy?" Then we iterate words—the thesaurus is your friend—and phrases until the client finds the thing that resonates with what they do.

If your gift is being a ballbuster, then be a ballbuster. There are certainly industries or spheres of influence where ballbusting is a huge asset (no pun intended). There may be certain situations where ballbusting is not required and can upset the apple cart; here, you might dial it back a bit. By leading authentically in every situation, however, you'll eventually find or create the right culture, one that embraces and needs ballbusters. You will be more successful and more comfortable because you're not turning yourself inside out to be something other than who you truly are. The only way to show up and lead authentically is to not judge your style or try to figure out if it's right or wrong. Simply own what is, and then you can figure out how to dial it up or down so your It Factor doesn't create problems for you.

I led teams for many years before I ever thought to assess my own authentic leadership. I had to be brutally honest with myself. Let's face it, the mirror doesn't always show us what we want to see. But it does show us what works. I had open conversations and took notes. I thought about the qualities I admire in others and then listed those I believe are part of who I am. I was also honest enough to put aside those traits I knew I admired but would never be able to embody. I thought about the sphere where I wanted to build influence, and then I put it all together. All the data point to leading with connection.

As this book makes apparent, communication is at the core of all my work, and the main reason is that communication is founded on connection. The desire to create connection leads me to engage with strangers, work to understand those who are different from me, and find common ground with anyone. It also shows up in my desire to mentor and help entrepreneurs build better connections with their stakeholders and to make introductions when I believe them to be of value. Connection shows up in everything I do. It is why my clients trust me and allow me to walk with them through this process.

The executive presence assessment in Chapter 3 provides another tool to help you assess your default style. The goal of that keyword assessment is to help you refine and leverage your authentic executive *presence*, which is one aspect of authentic leadership. When you go through the assessment, part of the process involves seeing where you are right now and part of it involves choosing words that describe where you want to be in a year. You choose certain words because you already feel a connection to them. If you reflect honestly on yourself, you will not choose words that are inauthentic to who you are.

Evolving that presence as your company or career grows can help you move closer to leading exclusively with your authentic leadership style.

SLOW DOWN TO SPEED UP

Once you've identified your authentic leadership style, consider how to leverage it. In rapidly growing organizations, and particularly when there is turbulence, lean on that authenticity. Doing so can help you engage teams, clarify decision making, and ensure the disruption isn't made worse with inauthenticity.

Your It Factor can guide you in authentically leading your organization through all the ups and downs of business. It is your foundation, your true north; it will show up in everything you do. Leverage it powerfully. Leaving your It Factor on a shelf or back at home is like failing to use your best and most powerful tool.

What is *your* It Factor? Embrace it, lean into it, and lead with it. Be authentically, unapologetically you.

TURBULENCE TOOLKIT

In each chapter, I have provided questions and suggestions to help you assess and manage unseen or unaddressed turbulence in your organization. I wish I could do that here. However, I have found that authentic leadership style is the most personal and specific work I do. It requires customized tools from my toolkit, which unfortunately, I can't provide here.

That said, here are a few things to keep in mind.

Assess

The more we know ourselves, the closer we get to showing up and leading authentically every day. In addition to the self-assessment tools in each chapter, you can use formal assessments such as the Myers-Briggs, Hogan, and StrengthsFinder. Too often, someone takes the assessment, scans the report, and throws it to the back of a drawer. The key to these formal assessments is to have someone well versed in them walk you through the results to help you understand how to leverage the insights.

Since time is at a premium, choose the assessment that best speaks your language and use the results daily. Also, remember that self-assessment is not a once-in-a-career thing. As your career progresses, new roles, challenges, and experiences will inform you authentic style. Incorporating those assessments into your growth plan can be fun if you are truly open to continual development.

Be Intentional

Choose to be intentional, both about identifying your authentic leadership style and living it out. It will likely feel exhausting at first, but if you slow down to speed up, being intentional should become easier.

Pick One Thing

- Identify your It Factor.
- Identify your authentic leadership style.
- Leverage your authentic leadership style.

Dig Deeper

- Clifton Strengths Finder: www.gallup.com/clifton-strengths/en/strengthsfinder.aspx
- Hogan Assessments: www.hoganassessments.com
- *Meditation for Fidgety Skeptics: A 10% Happier How-to Book* by Dan Harris, Jeffrey Warren, and Carlye Adle
- *Mirror Thinking: How Role Models Make Us Human* by Fiona Murden
- The Myers-Briggs Foundation: www.myersbriggs.org
- *The Power of Habit: Why We Do What We Do in Life and Business* by Charles Duhigg
- *Tiny Habits: The Small Changes That Change Everything* by BJ Fogg

CONCLUSION

"If you want things to be different, you have to do things differently."

—MONIQUE MALEY

No matter how long we've been in leadership roles, we all have blind spots and areas where we can grow, whether it's in our own career or in response to the needs of the organization. We constantly iterate as leaders based on experience, new factors, and what's required in new roles.

At the same time, there's a danger in trying to iterate in too many areas all at once. If you wanted to turn a company around, you wouldn't go in and change everything in one fell swoop, so don't put that burden on yourself.

My advice is to start with One Thing—The One Thing you want to know, think, do, or believe differently as a result of reading this book. If several areas come to mind, pick the one where streamlining turbulence will have the most immediate impact on you, your team, or your organization. In fact, pull out a Post-it note right now and write down your One Thing. Don't wait, don't think you'll do it later when you get back to the office.

Write it down and stick it on your wall or on your laptop—someplace where you will see it often and stay focused on it.

No matter where you start, the first step is the same: slow down and assess the source of turbulence. Then be intentional about how you move forward. Begin by trying one tool, implementing one change, or applying one strategy.

I also ask you to reframe your concept of *communication*. Approach it as the foundation of effective leadership and understand how and when it can be the solution to a problem.

The Work Institute calls communication the "dialect of leadership."[34] Every chapter of this book has highlighted a different area where poor, ineffective, or absent communication can create drag and disruption. The more quickly your organization changes and grows, the more apparent and often violent the turbulence.

For much of the last hundred years, heads of organizations have been directive, referred to as bosses, but the world of work is changing. Markets are ever evolving and less predictable. Competition can grow more quickly. Multigenerational employees require varied training and diverse modes of working. Teams don't want to be managed; they want to be led. Management books have given way to leadership books. Empathy and engagement are now words used in business.

This new work ecosystem is more human centered in which soft skills like empathy play a greater role. A 2019 article by

---

34   Work Institute, 2019 Retention Report (Franklin, TN: Work Institute, 2019), https://info.workinstitute.com/hubfs/2019%20Retention%20Report/Work%20Institute%202019%20Retention%20Report%20final-1.pdf.

McKinsey states, "Soft skills, which are commonly defined as non-technical skills that enable someone to interact effectively and harmoniously with others, are vital to organizations and can impact culture, mindsets, leadership, attitudes and behaviors."[35] Every soft skill listed in that article—advanced communication and negotiation skills, interpersonal skills and empathy, entrepreneurship and initiative-taking, adaptability and continuous learning skills, and teaching and training skills—inherently involves effective conversation and communication. Leaders who leverage the ability to "commune" at work will experience the most meaningful gains for employees and ultimately the organization's bottom line.

Affecting that type of change happens slowly at first, much like the ripples created when you throw a stone. This book began at the core of you as a leader and worked its way out to expanding spheres of influence. By the same token, if you refine the way you converse, engage, and influence, then you will create the first ripple. That ripple will create the next and so on. Once others see a leader effect change for the better, it informs the culture and others are inspired to do the same. Eventually, the whole organization will communicate more effectively. For me, that is the joy of leadership. Those are the ripples we can create.

I'm quite familiar with the tendency to buy a book like this, glance at it, and then put it on a shelf to collect dust. Resist that temptation. Instead, like a pilot trying to figure out how to streamline the jet, come back to this book for strategies or resources to mitigate the new disruptions that are sure to arise.

---

35 Julie Avrane-Chopard, Jamie Potter, and David Muhlmann, "How to Develop Softskills," McKinsey Organization Blog, November 11, 2019, https://www.mckinsey.com/business-functions/organization/our-insights/the-organization-blog/how-to-develop-soft-skills.

My hope is that each person takes away One Thing that allows them to engage more fully, articulate more clearly, and influence more authentically. If this happens for you, then this book has done its job, for the ripples will start moving ever outward.

BEGIN HERE

Here's a simple list to help you begin to end the turbulence.

1. Pick One Thing.
2. Write it on a Post-it.
3. Be intentional. Slow down and be intentional about how you can make changes in that area.
4. Get perspective. Look at resources. Read a variety of books by people who have different points of view on the same subject. Talk to your team. Once you identify a plausible source of the turbulence, get perspective from the people in your organization. Ask mentors and coaches. Ask someone who has no dog in the fight, someone who can simply put up a mirror without judgment. Doing so can get you where you're going faster.
5. Set metrics for yourself—indicators that you have made a shift. Each time you reach one of these sign-posts, that small win will motivate you to keep moving forward. It's the classic snowball effect. As you start showing up differently, people will start engaging with you differently, which creates ripples throughout the organization.
6. Hold yourself accountable. Whom are you going to tell? I say tell the whole world. If you tell everybody you know that you want to lose ten pounds, you will be far more likely to get up and go to the gym or stop yourself from eating those fries. If you don't tell anyone, there's no sense of accountability or motivation.
7. Remember that growing into an ever-more effective leader is a lifelong work. To me, this is the exciting part. We are always iterating as human beings, and we will always be iterating as leaders.
8. Once you feel like you have mastered that area of turbulence, pick another to address. Wash, rinse, repeat.

ACKNOWLEDGMENTS

As I finish this book, I must begin by thanking Gail Fay, my tireless and supportive editor. Her patience and encouragement made this crazy year a bit easier.

To Tucker Max, for his voice in my head, telling me to get off my ass and write my book. It took me longer than I would have liked, but I made it.

To Ron Kessler, my first coach, for being a great friend and constant inspiration.

To my dear friend and colleague Vishy Parameswaran, for listening ear, his collaboration, and his friendship.

To my awesome assistant, Casey Navarro. Without her support and backup, I could not have finished this book.

To Bella, I owe more than a thank-you for all the support, encouragement, and belief. She made this book possible in so many ways.

Finally, to all my amazing clients. Thank you for allowing me into your worlds and your work. Thank you for being open to our conversations. Thank you for the invaluable lessons I have learned from you all.

ABOUT THE AUTHOR

MONIQUE MALEY is a CEO, serial entrepreneur, and angel investor. In 2011, she founded Articulate Persuasion, her third entrepreneurial success and a company that cultivates authentic and influential leaders. As a classically trained actor with more than a decade spent in the theater and film industries, Monique offers her clients unique insight into influential communication. She leverages her actor's toolkit and entrepreneurial experience to mentor leaders with a distinctive approach that emphasizes adaptability, impactful communication, and connection with others. Monique's clients include *Fortune* 500 companies, complex government-funded organizations, and scrappy startups from around the world. Monique geeks out over Formula 1, Shakespeare, and her dogs, Mia and Archie. She currently lives in Washington, DC.